Also by Jude Ellison S. Doyle

*Trainwreck: The Women We Love
to Hate, Mock, and Fear . . . and Why*

*Dead Blondes and Bad Mothers: Monstrosity, Patriarchy, and the Fear
of Female Power*

Did
I Leave
Feminism?

dilf

Jude Ellison S. Doyle

MELVILLE HOUSE
BROOKLYN • LONDON

DILF

First published in 2025 by Melville House Publishing
Copyright © 2024 by Jude Ellison S. Doyle
All rights reserved
First Melville House Printing: July 2025
Distributed by Penguin Random House LLC,
1745 Broadway, New York, NY 10019 USA.
www.penguinrandomhouse.com

Melville House Publishing
46 John Street
Brooklyn, NY 11201
and
Melville House UK
Suite 2000
16/18 Woodford Road
London E7 0HA

mhpbooks.com
@melvillehouse

ISBN: 978-1-68589-215-9
ISBN: 978-1-68589-216-6 (eBook)

Library of Congress Control Number: 2025936968

Designed by Beste M. Doğan

Printed in the United States of America
10 9 8 7 6 5 4 3 2 1

A catalog record for this book is available from the Library of Congress

The authorized representative in the EU for product safety and
compliance is Easy Access System Europe, Mustamäe tee 50, 10621 Tallinn,
Estonia. gpsr.requests@easproject.com

For my family:
Thank you for buying this.
Please do not read it until I'm dead.

Males cannot love themselves
in patriarchal culture if their
very self-definition relies on
submission to patriarchal rules.
—bell hooks, *The Will to Change*

For queerness can never define an
identity; it can only ever disturb one.
—LEE EDELMAN, *No Future*

DID I LEAVE
FEMINISM?

What happens when a man takes
feminism utterly seriously, in every area of
his life, in every moment of everything
he does? Does he still stay a man?—or does
he turn into something else?
—JOHN STOLTENBERG

FOR MOST OF MY ADULT LIFE, MY JOB WAS TO BE A WOMAN.
In the fall of 2020, I quit my job.

I was a feminist author from the blog era, the beneficiary of a brief, strange trend that allowed anyone with an internet connection and a sufficient number of hot takes to declare themselves a Feminist Expert. I had a clear and coherent and highly rehearsed persona, and I had several centuries of previous feminist writing to guide me every time I sat down to write. I knew the issues and how to convey them, and what important things had already been said or written about them. Some people called me a man-hating identitarian boner-killer, and some people called me a heroic strong-female-character girlboss, but all of those people knew what box to put me in and where I fit in their world.

It made sense. *I* made sense—at least, I did to everyone but me. I firmly meant everything I said about feminism and misogyny and the necessity of smashing the patriarchy, and I stand by it. Yet I understood, on some deep-down level, that I was more miserable about being a woman than any woman I had ever met.

In time, I realized that my misery had a name, and that I could end it. I came out publicly as nonbinary, then as trans, then as a nonbinary trans man. And then, suddenly, nothing about me made sense anymore.

> "When you fail at being a woman so hard you decide to transition into a man, you don't get to comment anymore on feminism, femininity, or motherhood. You canceled your membership, dude."

> "I also like how she opted out of being a woman but still wants people to acknowledge that she's oppressed."

> "It also strikes me as intensely treacherous to be a feminist and then become a guy."

I collected internet comments like this for years after my transition. I found them everywhere. You could write all these people off as bigots—they mostly are—but the confusion followed me into my real life, into my relationships with readers and friends. Cis women I had known for decades dropped out of my life after my transition. "I felt so empowered to embrace my feminine strength [because of your book]," wrote one woman, "and seeing you choosing a masculine pronoun instead of a feminine one left me a bit puzzled."

Whether people loved me or hated me, whether they reviled me openly or quietly turned away, the message was the same: I had left feminism. I had left womanhood. I had abandoned my post, and I had let everybody down.

To me, though, it seemed clear that my transition was the *most* feminist thing I had done in my life, and perhaps the only feminist action that was truly aimed at liberation from patriarchal gender rather than slowly chipping away at the worst parts of patriarchy to make them livable. If feminism opposes gender stereotypes (which it does) and rejects traditional gender roles (which it does) and upholds bodily autonomy ("My body, my choice," etc., etc.) then what could be more feminist than rejecting our system of assigned gender and remolding your body to fit the person you knew yourself to be?

Every day, my gender politics made more and more sense to me, and less and less sense to everyone around me. It used to be my job to explain feminist theory, and maybe it still was, but now, I was the one problem I simply could not explain.

———

TRANSMASCULINE PEOPLE ARE one of feminism's biggest blind spots. No one knows quite what to do with us, so it's easier to pretend we're not there. Books on "male feminism" or "feminist men" mostly teach men how to be allies to women's struggle—the idea that there might be men who actually *experience* pregnancy, or abortion, or being cat-called or sexually harassed or pay-gapped or any of the other things we traditionally call "women's issues" is not accounted for. Books on trans feminism understandably stress the importance of feminism for trans *women*, which is important, what with them being women and all, but do tend to reinforce the assumption that feminism is just for girls.

I'm hardly the first trans guy to run into this problem, or to write about it. The poet Cameron Awkward-Rich famously compared the relationship between *trans* and *feminist* to the one between Peter Pan and Wendy: They love each other, they need each other, but they can never quite merge, as lovers long to do. In order to be themselves, trans men must slip out of feminism's charmed circle, but they must also perpetually return to feminism in order to understand their lives. Even as he leaves the sisterhood, Awkward-Rich says, the transmasculine person knows that "there is, as of now, no better discourse he can speak to articulate the harms he incurred for failing to be [female]."[1]

Somewhat more hopefully, author and journalist Thomas Page McBee conceives of transmasculinity as an incentive and invitation to solidarity. "People sometimes think that being trans means I live 'between' worlds, but that's not exactly true," McBee says. "If anything, it has just created within me a potential for empathy that I must work every day, like a muscle, to grow."[2] He will never be a woman, and he doesn't automatically "get" what women are going through, but he can treat women with the dignity and respect he would have wanted, back when people mistook him for female.

This is all good stuff, great in fact—and yet I still see so much longing and lostness, confusion and frustration, whenever trans guys talk about feminism. Is this still, you know, *our thing*? Do we belong here? If feminism is no longer for us, are we being punished for "defecting" or "becoming the oppressor"? If it used to be for us—if our bodies and histories are still undeniably marked by the way the world treats people it regards as "women"—then what does it mean to lose feminism's protection? Do we still matter? Who's got our backs?

I saw some guys crumble into bitterness and start muttering about "misandry"; others fell into an apologetic cringe and never stopped reassuring the world they were Not Like Other Men; some guys, most guys, just retreated into themselves, and stopped saying much at all.

Meanwhile, in the abyss created by ignorance, monsters spawned. In 2025, the only self-proclaimed feminists who *do* spend a lot of time talking about transmasculine people are doing it with the intention of wiping us off the map.

TERFs—"trans-exclusive radical feminists," sometimes rebranded as "gender-critical," though their refusal to criticize traditional gender constructs is one very large part of the problem—are confident that they know exactly where transmasculine people fit in feminism: We're the enemy. TERFs believe that we hate women, and hate ourselves for being women, and that we are abandoning womanhood because our internalized misogyny leads us to believe we are better than other girls—*so* much better that we deserve to be treated as men, the Rolls-Royce of traditional gender options.

WHY THIS ISN'T A BOOK ABOUT TRANS INCLUSION

Traditionally, when we talk about trans people in feminism, we talk about "trans-exclusive" feminisms—the TERF kind—and "trans-inclusive" feminisms, the kind we like. However, as many trans people have pointed out, this framing is somewhat transphobic in its own right. "Inclusion" is what an insider does for an outsider, or a host does for a guest, as in, "I am including you on the invitation list for my birthday party." It implies that cis women own feminism and are letting other people into it. True acceptance is not "inclusion." It's knowing that this was never only your party.

Not only is this strand of feminism traditionally hostile to transmasculine people, feminism is promoted as the cure for transmasculinity. "Female-to-constructed-male transsexuals are relatively rare," wrote Janice Raymond, in *The Transsexual Empire*—the infamous codifying document of second-wave TERFism, sort of the Old Testament for hating trans people—and this is because "women have had a political outlet, that is, feminism, which has helped change the distribution of power for women in society and challenge sex role rigidification."[3]

For decades, this has been the line: Think you're a dude? Just be a feminist! But to be a feminist, *and* a dude, is impossible. All trans men are betraying feminism's promise, pursuing the selfish "individual" solution of transition over the work of changing gender stereotypes for the culture at large.

The language of "opting out," of "betraying" women, of aspiring to "male privilege" or opportunistically upgrading my gender the way you might upgrade from economy to first class on a long flight—all of that is coming from the TERFs, even if it has obtained alarmingly wide circulation. It is meant to discredit transmasculine people in the public sphere by casting our transness as inherently malicious. It's also meant to inspire transmasculine people to doubt *themselves*, to wonder if they really are being greedy or selfish or sexist by pursuing lives that don't make them utterly miserable every second of every day.

When I looked like a woman, I had a hundred experts telling me how to be a feminist. Now that I was visible as a man, I had almost none, and of the few that I could find, an alarming proportion of them thought I shouldn't exist. A wise man once said that you either die the hero or live long enough to see yourself become the villain. I had already become a man. In order to fill the absence I felt now, I would have to become the worst kind of man, the kind that had always annoyed the ever-living Christ out of me: A man who writes a book explaining feminism.

You know. *To women.*

Yikes.

———

I AM A feminist. I could never be anything else. I don't believe you can understand anything about gender unless you start from feminist theory—in a patriarchy, gender is always articulating a position within a hierarchy, and that hierarchy is violently unfair. Lose sight of that and you lose the plot.

I also believe transmasculine people need feminism. Maybe there will come a time when all trans people are allowed to figure out their gender in early childhood and transition so early that we have no memories of living in the wrong gender—but that is strikingly unlikely to happen anytime soon. Until we reach that future, most transmasculine people will spend at least part of their lives being mistaken for girls or women. Furthermore, as long as we live in a misogynist culture, the very fact of being *connected* to women, of having body parts or mannerisms or experiences that people think of as feminine, will be used as a reason to down-rank us, discriminate against us, and target us for violence.

Finally, I think feminism has room for transmasculine people, just as it has room and utility for transfeminine ones. You don't need to build trans people a new wing within feminism or put us up in an apartment over the garage; we were here at its beginning, and some of the earliest feminist texts are open to us, useful to us, in ways you might not expect. A lot of trans-exclusionary radical feminism irritates me, not just as transphobia, but *as feminism*—it is lazy, shallow, unimaginative; it evinces a poor understanding of the texts it cites. The biological determinism and neo-Victorian worship of white feminine fragility you'll find among today's "gender-criticals" would have been anathema to, say, second-wave radical feminist Shulamith Firestone, who famously said that even if gender *was* connected to biology, she didn't give a fuck: Humans had developed technology and medicine explicitly so that they could ignore biology when it conflicted with their needs.

"To grant that the sexual imbalance of power is biologically based is not to lose our case," she said. "We are no longer just animals. And the kingdom of nature does not reign absolute."[4]

To the extent that mainstream feminism is transphobic, it is because it's fallen out of touch with those impulses—it has refused to interrogate gender critically enough, radically enough, to get outside of the Western patriarchal gender binary.

THE WAVE WE WERE

Though this book's source materials are often from the second wave, its origins are in the third. *Whipping Girl*, by Julia Serano, came out in 2007; it's a core text of transfeminism, and remains many people's first introduction to the concept.

Serano tells me her book was possible because she came up in feminism's third wave. Second-wave feminism had a bad habit of assuming that the default feminist perspective was white, middle-class, and cisgender, and that everyone else was an addendum or a deviation from the norm. The third wave countered that by uplifting multiple marginalized perspectives to expand our ideas of what "the female experience" could be.

"I was coming up in a world where it was really obvious that there were multiple different strands of feminism," Serano says. "And so the idea was try to understand them and make sense through it and maybe some of it you think is right, and others you think are wrong in particular ways."

That diversity of thought has flattened out substantially in the past few years, particularly in the UK, where mainstream liberal feminism has now been associated almost exclusively with TERFs.

"If you're in the UK and you're growing up

right now, everything that's about feminism is about being anti-trans," Serano says. "The loudest voices online, like 'feminism, feminism, feminism,' it's all 'keeping men out of women's sports' and 'men in women's prisons' and everything. And I can understand why some younger people maybe think, well, that means feminism is bad."

If elder millennial and Gen X trans folks—like me, like Serano—are more comfortable with identifying as feminist than younger ones, it's precisely because we are more likely to remember a mainstream pop feminism that wasn't obsessively transphobic. The long arc of history bent away from justice, and it's on us to bend it back.

What follows is a series of attempts to knit my feminist past and trans present together, to figure out where I've been and where I might be going. I will warn you in advance that I am not the transmasculine Lorax; there are trans guys who aren't feminists, trans guys who are sexist, trans guys who think identity politics are a distraction and we should all just focus on ending capitalism, trans guys who are better feminists than me.

There are trans people who *aren't even guys*, if you can believe it: Trans women and transfeminine people have their own fraught history with feminism. I will never know what it's like to be transfeminine, and I've tried to focus on my own experience precisely so that I can avoid the trap of becoming a Confident White Man who assumes he speaks for everybody. Still, it's weird to call yourself a feminist if you don't actually talk to women; I have tried to interview trans women and transfeminine people throughout the book, so you can see outside and around my own relatively privileged perspective.

I do believe there are things to be seen from where I'm standing. Chicana feminist Gloria Anzaldúa famously wrote about being stuck between two identities: "I have so internalized the borderland conflict that sometimes I feel like one cancels out the other and we are zero, nothing, no-one." The border Anzaldua described was geographical—she lived where Texas met Mexico—but not only. In the same book, she wrote about her gender identity as "half and half," both male and female: "Half and halfs are not suffering from a confusion of sexual identity, or even from a confusion of gender," she wrote. "What we are suffering from is an absolute despot duality that says we are only able to be one or the other."[5]

Like Anzaldua, like so many of us, I need my bothness. I need my transness and my feminism to be compatible, because I would lose half of myself in losing either one. Having two homelands can mean being nothing and no one, but it can also mean having the capacity to connect people. I am stranded between two places, but so is a bridge. So is a pathway. So is a door.

I believe that feminism, like everything, is better when it can continually expand its horizons. So, here we are. Walk through this door with me. Let's see what's out there, in the world beyond what we know.

Part 1

GENDER

I don't feel like a man trapped in a
woman's body. I just feel trapped.

—LESLIE FEINBERG

I'VE SEEN THE INSIDE OF A PLANNED PARENTHOOD MORE
often as a man than I ever did when I was trying to be a woman.
On the morning that I want to begin this story, I'm sitting in the
lobby, waiting to be taught how to inject testosterone.

Every story about transition starts here: Men marveling at the
oily miracle of the fluid, bursting into tears in their doctors' offices, shouting "I did it" as they withdraw the needle. Those are
just the anecdotes. There's high literature to contend with: Maggie

Nelson in *The Argonauts*, telling Harry Dodge that "each time I count the four rungs down on the blue ladder tattooed on your lower back, spread out the skin, push in the nearly-two-inch-long needle, and plunge the golden, oily T into deep muscle mass, I feel certain I am delivering a gift."[1]

I am not going to cry, or if I do, it isn't going to be from happiness. For one thing, the narrative is all wrong. I've actually been on testosterone—a low-dose gel that cured my lifelong depression, gave me a new sense of peace within myself, and made no changes to my appearance whatsoever—for over a year. I'm switching to the needle because I've found, to my surprise, that the physical changes really do matter to me, and injecting is more likely to bring them. So I'm not starting testosterone. I'm starting to *look* like I've started testosterone. Even I, with my talent for wholly unnecessary drama, can't quite make that sing.

This brings me to the second problem: All those other transition stories feature a loving, benevolent, gender-affirming partner—a girlfriend; a wife; my designated Maggie Nelson, replacing the creaky boards of my ship—and I was told to bring my husband to this appointment, so that he could learn how to administer the shot. When we got there, COVID regulations had been changed, and he wasn't allowed in the building.

So there he is, out in the parking lot, waiting for me to have my miracle. Here I am, doing this on my own.

What I'm thinking about, moments before my joyous encounter with a nearly two-inch-long needle, is a Christopher Pike novel that I read in middle school. In that novel, the killer managed to commit "the perfect murder" by leaving one single air bubble in a syringe before an injection. When the air bubble passed through the victim's aorta, it stopped their heart: No struggle, no evidence, no one but the previous victim's vengeful ghost (I think?) to make things right. I have thought about Christopher Pike every single time I've had a needle pointed at me for the past thirty years, and those were pointed by doctors and nurses; they would be smart enough to *intentionally* murder me, whereas I'm pretty sure I could just fuck up and kill myself.

I wonder what's going to happen if I perfect-murder myself trying to transition. I wonder if they'll blame it on my husband, because he was supposed to give me the shot. I flash on every terrible true-crime documentary I've ever seen where *the perfect marriage became . . . the perfect murder!!!* and I try to envision a camera panning over our wedding photos in time with the voice-over, and then I realize that I don't want anyone seeing our wedding photos, because I'm not in them. I realize that not looking like a nice white lady means I probably can't star in true crime anymore.

Do men think about true crime documentaries? Are men scared of needles? Do men need to bring their husbands with them to doctors' appointments, like a four-year-old lugging around a teddy bear? (Men aren't supposed to have husbands.) Do men even read Christopher Pike books? A man wrote them, but that says nothing. I spend so much time thinking about what men are allowed to do these days. Half of my internal monologue is composed of questions that start with *Do men ____?* or *Are men supposed to _____?*

Do I want to be the kind of man who cares what men are supposed to do? No, right? Yet it's become very important to me that I have all the same feelings as a real—no, I mean a normal—no, I mean a *cisgender* man, is what I'm supposed to mean. If I can't be exactly like all the men who are nothing like me, if I can't prove that every last inch of me is 100 percent normatively and conclusively masculine, then it means I'm faking, and if I'm faking, then someone will find out and make me stop.

To be trans, I have to be happy. To be trans, I have to be sure. But I have never been sure about any important decision. I almost passed out from fear during my own wedding. I took over ten years to settle on the design for my first tattoo. Half of the internet is telling me that people who medically transition will end up dead or in prison camps within the next decade, and the other half is telling me that people who do this are sick, that we have some kind of self-mutilation fetish, or that we've gone mad from experiencing the sheer awfulness of sexism, which (I admit) I often think I have.

How is anyone supposed to be sure under these conditions? How do you ever shut the world out long enough to hear yourself think? It's easier to worry about the air bubble. Because here is the truth: Even as I'm sitting here, spiraling toward a Christopher Pike–brand panic attack, I know that I'm going to do this. No matter how scared I am, or how hard I try to talk myself out of transitioning, I just *know*. It's as if it's already happened; some future version of me has traced the track and I'm just following him, waiting to catch up.

Maybe this is what certainty feels like. Maybe I just don't recognize it, because it's never happened: being scared, but still being sure.

———

THIS IS A book about gender—what it is, what it means, what it does to us in our daily lives. It will help if we define our terms. When we use the word "gender," we are actually talking about at least three separate but heavily overlapping systems: Gender as an identity, gender as a language, and gender as a political system of control. When we confuse or overlook these distinctions, conflict happens. Here, then, in three definitions and two detours, is an attempt to define what we talk about when we talk about "gender."

#1

GENDER AS AN IDENTITY

("I'VE ALWAYS BEEN A MAN.")

YOU HAVE A GENDER. YOU ALSO HAVE AN *ASSIGNED* GEN-der, which a doctor likely pinned on you when you were born by checking out your genital configuration. Most people grow up to find out that their lived gender roughly aligns with their assigned one—we call them *cisgender,* or *cis,* from a Latin word that means "on this side." A substantial portion of the population will find out that their gender does not align with their assignment. Some experience this as a visceral, agonizing sense of their body's wrongness; for others, it's more like a diffuse sensation that something is off. (It's hard to know what the "wrong" gender feels like when you've never lived in the "right" one.) In any case, people who need to correct their genders are called *transgender*—*trans* being Latin for "on the other side," as in, you had to cross over to get where you were going.

Despite what the "trans" vs. "cis" binary would imply, there are not only two sides. There are not only two genders, either. Some trans people need to transition medically or socially, and some don't; different trans people often require different forms of treatment; some of us are men, some are women, some are both or neither or something else. Intersex people do exist and are about as common in the population as natural redheads. "Trans" is a useful umbrella term for people who aren't cisgender, but "the world" is a useful term for every place that isn't your house. The outside is bigger and more varied than the inside, in both cases.

Gender diversity has existed in every society throughout human history. In ancient Rome, there were the Galli, priestesses of the goddess Cybele who ritually removed their penises and wore feminine dress. The Vikings told stories of male gods who gave birth and women who turned into kings; at least one stereotypically "male" warrior's grave was discovered, in 2017, to contain "female" bones.[2]

Trans people exist everywhere and in every time. We exist whether or not we're allowed to exist. Our existence is not "socially constructed," because we exist in societies that do not comprehend or construct us. Once you become aware of trans people's historical existence, it becomes hard not to see us everywhere— even in something as random and seemingly unrelated as *Wisconsin Death Trip*, a collection of news items from rural Wisconsin in the nineteenth century, where you can find the following 1894 scandal:

> Anna Morris, alias Frank Blunt, the woman who has
> tried to be a man for the last 15 years was arrested and
> sent to the penitentiary for one year . . . she was arrested
> several months ago in Milwaukee, charged with stealing
> $175 . . . It was then discovered that the prisoner was
> a woman, although she had worn masculine attire
> nearly all her life . . . after the sentence had been passed,
> Gertrude Field, a woman who claimed to have married
> the prisoner in Eau Claire, fell upon the neck of the
> prisoner and wept for half an hour. This woman has
> furnished all the money for Blunt's defense and now
> proposes to carry the case to the Supreme Court.

This isn't the only story about a trans person in nineteenth-century America. In fact, it's not even the only story in *Wisconsin Death Trip*. In Kenosha, a society woman known as Mrs. Howe organized a church benefit and was later revealed to be male-assigned at birth. Mrs. Howe was a respectable lady, and "the peculiarity of her manners was commented on at the time, but none suspected the real truth."[3] Frank Blunt and Mrs. Howe are clearly included in *Wisconsin Death Trip* as examples of "strange" news—we're meant to gawk at them, not empathize—but plenty of other newspaper stories throughout history, maybe even throughout this one book, were about trans people. We just don't know that, because they weren't outed.

This is all to say: Despite what you may have heard, being trans is not a recent phenomenon or a trend. Nor is it a mere reaction to present-day gender roles. Some people have always been trans, and some people always will be, because transness appears to be innate—it's something you just are, whether you like it or not.

It is this level of gender that trans people refer to when we say things like "I've always been a man." Although gender is a mystery in many ways, it seems to be intrinsic to most people's sense of self. In *Whipping Girl*, Julia Serano refers to this as "subconscious sex," and she points out that, if it weren't a powerful force, people would change genders whenever it was convenient. "Gender studies grad students would transition for a few years to gather data for their theses. Actors playing transsexuals would go on hormones for a few months to make their portrayals more authentic."[4]

Honestly, the grad student thing doesn't sound like a bad idea to me. Yet it doesn't happen, because most people resist it in some deep and instinctive way. The idea of waking up in the "wrong" body feels bad and scary. One of my favorite examples comes from the deeply transphobic cis photographer Laura Dodsworth, describing how creeped out she is by transmasculine bodies: "For me, the idea of having my breasts, ovaries, and womb removed, and then wanting them back, creates a feeling so unnerving I cannot occupy it for long."[5]

Of course, that indelible wrongness is also what many trans men feel when they wake up *with* breasts and a uterus. In attempting to debunk their gender identity, Dodsworth has inadvertently confirmed her own. You are attached to your gender, not in the way you're attached to a partner or a pet dog, but in the way you're attached to your teeth—you may not think about them often, but if someone tried to rip them out, it would hurt.

#2

GENDER AS A LANGUAGE

("MEN'S CLOTHING SECTION.")

GENDER IS NOT JUST A PERSONAL EXPERIENCE. IT'S A social phenomenon. It's not enough to know you are a man or a woman; other people must also know this about you, and in order to make that happen, you need to communicate your gender to the world.

The traditional conception of trans people doesn't go any further than this second layer: Trans people are people who dress up in the "wrong" gender's signifiers. This is why transphobic commentators often accuse trans people of confusing gender stereotypes with gender identities—thinking that wearing lipstick is the same thing as being female, or that liking soccer is the same thing as being a boy. "'Woman' is not a costume,"[6] quoth J. K. Rowling.

Of course, the world contains lipstick-wearing men and soccer-playing women; Robert Smith and Megan Rapinoe are not unknown to my people. For that matter, there are plenty of cis people with exaggerated or stereotypical gender presentations: Clint Eastwood, Marilyn Monroe, female ballerinas, male NFL quarterbacks, etc. Yet transgender presentations receive extra scrutiny, often a cruelly double-edged variety: If trans people conform to traditional gender norms, we're "reinforcing stereotypes." If trans people are gender nonconforming—and many of us are—then we're "not passing," which makes us freaks. At all times, the assumption is that we are playing dress-up, imitating cis people, who set the standards for what is real.

Yet *everyone* is playing dress-up in their gender, whether they are trans or not. Even if "woman" is not a costume, you have to wear the right costume in order for people to know that you're a woman. As a culture, we have an array of signs and symbols and, yes, stereotypes that signify gender, and we have to incorporate them into our presentations—not because those symbols and stereotypes are objectively true, but because, otherwise, people won't be able to guess what gender we're trying to put across.

I will show you what I mean. Take a moment, right now, and draw two stick figures. Make one of them male and one of them female. Do it on the side of the page, on the cover, on a notepad, whatever you can get your hands on, but don't read anything else until you're finished drawing. Got it?

Now: If you are like most people, your "female" stick figure has a little skirt, and maybe long hair, if you're feeling crafty. Your male stick figure has been allowed to rest comfortably bald and nude—given the vagaries of stick figure fashion, we can never be sure he's not wearing pants.

Of course, you know that not all women wear skirts, just as you know there are men with long hair. You didn't draw your stick figures this way because you're a hardened misogynist, you did it because symbols are less complex than reality. Long hair is not a woman, but long hair *means* woman in the language of gender.

It's true that our ideas of what "men" look like tend to change over the years. In seventeenth-century France, you could identify a manly man by his high heels, silken tights, and long, flowing curls; in 1980s America, hypermasculine hair metal bands wore lip gloss and glitter eye shadow. Behavioral standards change: "Boys don't cry," for example, is a new one. In *The Iliad,* Greek and Trojan soldiers alternate between dismembering each other and breaking down into messy, public tears. I was taught that straight men should never touch each other—even in a movie theater, you had to leave an empty seat between you and your bro, lest you brush hands and accidentally become gay in the middle of *Saw 7.* In parts of the Middle East, I'm told, male friends often casually hold hands while walking down the street, and there are no sexual connotations.

But you're not trying to pass as a seventeenth-century aristocrat or a member of Whitesnake, are you? You're trying to use the men's room in a Target without being kicked out. Thankfully, you and everyone else in that men's room already share an idea of what a "man's" haircut and or a "man's" outfit looks like, one so simple and widely shared that you can take it more or less for granted.

This is gender as a language: Not an eternal truth, or an essential quality, but something you can use to communicate with the world.

THE OBLIGATORY PART WHERE WE TALK ABOUT JUDITH BUTLER

All of this is similar to what Judith Butler meant when they famously declared gender to be "performative." Unfortunately, most people nowadays use the word "performative" to mean "fake." That's not what Butler meant—for them, "performative" is an utterance that creates reality, like stamping an "M" or an "F" on a birth certificate, or saying "I now pronounce you man and wife" at a wedding—but the confusion inadvertently feeds into the misconception that trans people are "pretending" to be who we are.

The concept of gender as a language is one I've found in the work of transfeminist Susan Stryker: "I see gender as the language through which you communicate the reality of your identifications and desires to other people," she has said. "Not just verbally and visually, but with your whole body, in a language of movement and smell and sound."*

I like this metaphor, because a language is learned, not innate—you're not born knowing French or Spanish or white Western masculinity—but you typically acquire at least one language when you're very young, by watching and listening to the people around you. You're not *deceiving* other people by translating your thoughts and feelings into words; you're just doing the work of making them understandable. Language, like gender performance, is culturally constructed and also necessary; something artificial that we use to communicate what is real.

---

* "Another Dream of a Common Language: An Interview with Sandy Stone," Susan Stryker, *Transgender Studies Quarterly*, Vol. 3, Nos. 1–2, May 2016.

This might seem low-stakes or frivolous: What kind of feminist spends a whole section of a book defining appropriate hairstyles? However, knowing your society's acceptable gender expressions can be a matter of life and death. The boundaries of gender are patrolled with violence, and the more obviously gender nonconforming you are, the higher your risk. Trans people often obsess over the finer details of gender signaling—how you use your hands, how you stand, who you make eye contact with, how you pitch your voice at the end of sentences—because being able to clearly and accurately convey our gender, and fulfill other people's gendered expectations, is what keeps us safe.

An example: I was going through a maze recently with my six-year-old daughter. She got away from me, and I sped up to catch her. As I rounded a corner, I nearly bumped into a woman—about my own age, a little bit shorter than me—who recoiled away from me so hard she hit the opposite wall, clutched her chest, and, pointing me out to her companion, gasped, "This guy!"

This is a pretty common experience for trans guys: We don't fully realize that we look like cis men until women start reacting to us like we're Jason Voorhees. Now, I mean this woman no harm, but in order to communicate that, I need to be fluent in gender.

I know, for instance, that many women experience real fear when a man intrudes on their personal space, and that some women carry terrible memories; she's not overreacting, and being surprised by "some lady" probably wouldn't provoke the same reaction. She may already be mentally rehearsing her set of responses to a dangerous man, trying to figure out how to repel me without getting hurt. I also know that this situation is dangerous for me—cis women are just as likely as cis men to be transphobic, and to enforce their transphobia with violence. (Consider the infamous "bathroom problem," wherein butch women are routinely harassed or accosted for using the women's restroom.) If this woman realizes I'm trans, her fear could result in me being assaulted or kicked out before I find my kid.

For both of us, reestablishing safety relies on finding some quick and obvious way to signify that I am not a threat. This is not as easy as you'd think. Certain responses that would have read as comforting or maternal prior to my transition—reaching out a hand to steady her, calling her "hon" when I ask if she's okay—would come across as intrusive or scary now. Thus, I decide not to prolong our interaction, but to simply demonstrate respect for her space, which I do by saying "sorry," backing up, and giving her a wide berth as she walks past me. I look at the ground to avoid making eye contact. I hold my hands up, so she can see them, the entire time.

I don't think it's wildly sexist for me to acknowledge the realities of male violence, or to take those realities into account when being polite to strangers. I also don't think it's anti-feminist to minimize my own odds of being attacked. To accomplish either of those things, though, I have to refer to an internal rolodex of stereotypes, both the ones I want to abide by (men don't touch strangers; men don't use terms of endearment without sexual intent) and the ones I want to defy (men are predators; men are bullies; men careen through the world like circus elephants that have snapped their tethers, trampling all in their path; and so on).

If this is still hard to swallow, consider that we signal our identities on many fronts, not just gender. Take another look at your bald, nude stick man: What sort of man is he, this hairless enigma? Is he an artist? A chef? Is he, perhaps, the Judge from

Cormac McCarthy's *Blood Meridian*, for whom baldness and nudity—along with a profound and ageless evil that represents, I think, American imperialism—are the defining parts of his presentation? There's simply no way to tell under the present conditions. So, if you don't want your stick man to stand for all the depravity of conquest, you had better draw a little firefighter's hat on him and fix him in some more noble profession.

"Woman" is a costume. "Man" is a costume. *"Firefighter" is a costume*. We are all constantly calibrating our presentations to show the world who we are, or who we want to be. Yet, when we do it with gender, people get anxious. The question I want to answer is why. To get there, though, we have to take a detour.

Detour

"SOCIALIZATION"

ANY DISCUSSION OF GENDER HAS TO MENTION SOCIAL-ization at some point. Unfortunately, "socialization," as it's levied against trans people, is used in bad faith, to imply that we can't be trusted or that we are not the people we say we are. The paradigmatic example is cis feminists claiming that trans women are "pushy" or "aggressive" because of their "male socialization," whereas a cis woman who showed similar assertiveness would most likely be applauded for *overcoming* her "female socialization" to "stand up for herself" or "take up space."

This version of socialization rests on a few assumptions:

- Everyone receives either "male socialization" or "female socialization" depending on their assigned gender. Children assigned male at birth (AMAB for short) don't receive female socialization, and children assigned female (AFAB) cannot be socialized male.

- Male socialization and female socialization work the same way for everybody—that is, all AMAB and AFAB people are taught to be men and women in roughly the same way, with roughly the same results.

- Socialization is a one-time process that occurs in childhood. You are taught how to be your assigned gender and set loose, never to be socialized again.

- Socialization is determinative. The way you are socialized in childhood always determines who you are and how you behave as an adult—you cannot be or act "male" if you were "female socialized," and vice versa.

All of these assumptions are wrong. "There is no singular 'female socialization,' no universal afab or amab experience," writes social psychologist Devon Price, "and it harms all of us to pretend that there is."

Take the first assumption—that we all either get male or female socialization, that we are taught the rules for "our" gender and not the other. In a binary system, genders don't occur in isolation; they are mirror-flipped images of each other, so that learning to act "like a girl" is also learning *not* to act like a boy, and vice versa.

"We all grow up in a cissexist world, which teaches us that a person's body determines how they are supposed to dress, which bathroom they are to use, who they're allowed to hang out with, and what they should aspire to in life," Price writes. "We learn these expectations for *both* binary genders, and we witness how failure to conform to either role is penalized."

So you learn the rules for both patriarchal genders, no matter which one you are sorted into. Even so, definitions of "masculinity" and "femininity" can vary wildly, depending on race, class, culture, or any number of other intersecting identities, and the socialization you receive will depend on where and how you are raised.

In our conversation, Price pointed to his own experience of growing up working-class: "The expectation that assigned female people be feminine is, like, not even a thing if you're from a working-class family," Price told me. "The ideal woman to be was strong, capable, had physical skills, was not interested in feminine frivolity, anything like that. Femininity can be forbidden even if you're quote-unquote 'female.'"

Middle-class people are taught that men are breadwinners; working-class people are taught that everybody has to pull their weight. A white boy is raised to see manhood as his access to power; a Black boy knows that manhood means being seen as a criminal and a brute, and potentially being executed by a cop based on that stereotype. There's no monolithic "male" or "female" socialization that applies across all contexts. Women of color are socialized differently than white women, working-class women are socialized differently than wealthy women, and trans women are socialized differently than cis women, but it would take a bigot to construe all that diversity as a failure to achieve the norm.

Finally, even if we acknowledge the wide range of male and female socializations—if we say that a Muslim girl in Park Slope, Brooklyn, is socialized differently from an evangelical Christian girl in rural Nevada—we must also factor in that socialization is an ongoing process. If our evangelical girl leaves home and moves to Los Angeles, she will learn and internalize a whole new set of gendered rules.

We are socialized and resocialized continually throughout our lifetimes: We learn to be children, then young adults, then middle-aged, and then elders, with different expectations and privileges at each step. ("Teenagers who rebelled against the authority of adults grow up to become adults with authority, who wield that authority against teens," to quote Price's essay again.[7]) We are socialized into different social classes, as we ascend or descend the ladder; we are socialized into different regions, different subcultures, different jobs.

Even if you assume that I received "female socialization" growing up, and that it affected me the same way it would affect a cis girl—which you shouldn't—I also started receiving "male socialization" the second I looked legibly male. One way or another, trans people often wind up having the same gendered hang-ups as cis people; I've spoken to trans women who have trouble asserting themselves and tend to slip into caretaking roles in their relationships. Price himself participates in the greatest of all masculine rituals, the quasi-annual Butching It Up Around the Repairman.

"Right now, I'm having to book some drywall getting fixed in my house," Price tells me. "And nothing makes me feel emasculated quite like talking to these big Chicago guys who know how to fix things . . . I'm like, who am I trying to kid, the way I'm carrying myself and the way I'm lowering my voice? They know I don't know what the fuck the difference is between drywall and plaster. They're still going to rip me off."

We are all constantly taught how to "be a man" or "be a woman," and we are all constantly in danger of failing. To say that trans people's gender is no less natural than cis people's is also to say that cis people's gender is no less learned than ours.

Finally, the socialization argument rests on the assumption that trans children receive the same gendered socialization as cis ones—which we don't. The one unavoidable fact about trans children is that *they're trans*, and often exhibit some degree of gender nonconformity growing up, which is all too often met with abuse. Raising a child to suppress her femininity and "act like a boy" is very different from raising a boy who has no femininity to speak of, and two very different children will result. This is why it's often said that trans people aren't socialized male or female; trans people are socialized trans, and even that can look very different, depending on who you're talking to.

So, sure: "Socialization" can be useful in terms of interpreting large-scale social patterns (men *on average* are more likely to speak up more during the meeting, though not all do; women *on average* do more housework, though not all do, etc.) but it is spectacularly bad at predicting the behavior of individual human beings.

"Nobody believes socialization works the way that they imply when it comes to the assumption that I was 'male socialized,' and that it has permanently affected me, and I can never overcome it," Julia Serano says. "It's like, well, why aren't we all perfect, straight, gender-conforming people then?"

If socialization made people incapable of deviating from the norms for their assigned gender, not only would there be no trans people—there would be no feminists. When building solidarity between groups, it helps to focus less on *socialization* and more on *marginalization*: Not some quasi-mystical fund of shared experience, which never really existed, but the very material, very real oppression being stamped down on all of us from above.

Detour

MARGINALIZATION

"A WOMAN'S BODY BELONGS NOT ONLY TO HER, BUT TO mankind," writes philosopher-novelist Olga Tokarczuk. "Since she gives birth, she's public property . . . at the same time as being herself, a woman belongs to us all."[8]

Tokarczuk's statement, simplistic though it may be, does accurately sum up the past several centuries of gender discourse: In patriarchy, women do not own or control their own bodies. Women are a class of people that men use for sex, for childbirth, for domestic labor, and sometimes for comfort and companionship (this last tends to happen whether the women like it or not). Rape, domestic violence, workplace sexual harassment, and the criminalization of abortion and birth control are all ways that men appropriate women's bodies and exercise social and political power over them.

Yet not all women give birth. Not all women even have uteruses—but we are no kinder to them, in the long run. You do not have to be a childbearing cis woman to have a body that is considered public, or to have harsh state and social control imposed on your body, because patriarchy is not set up to punish and control *women* so much as it is set up to oppress anyone who is *not* a cis white man.

In February 2023, I watched nonbinary transmasculine activist Lindsey Spero inject T in front of the Florida board of medicine. Spero spoke before the board after almost three hours of testimony from trans people, begging the board not to ban gender-affirming care for minors. Spero took the shot because they knew the care was going to be banned no matter what those people said.

"I could sit here and tell you about the times I tried to end my life because I didn't have access to gender-affirming care," Spero told the board, "but I know. I know you don't care."[9] Instead of speaking, they pulled their shirt up, took the cap of a syringe off with their teeth, and injected the T into their abs, as the medical board watched in stunned silence. The whole thing took less than a minute.

Like most people, I caught the clip when trans journalist Alejandra Caraballo posted it online. The first time I watched it, Spero's action seemed brilliant: De-mythologizing the endlessly mythologized process of transition, forcing their audience to realize that all the furor and handwringing and legislation had been directed at an ordinary medical procedure taking place in an ordinary fluorescent-lit room.

Years later, Spero still seems brilliant, but the gesture itself has gotten much sadder. In the United States, 125 anti-trans bills had been filed by the fifth day of January 2024.[10] Every year since 2020 has been a record-breaking year for anti-trans legislation; every year brings more bans than any previous year. While I was finishing the final draft of this book, the first piece of federal legislation banning transition care—the National Defense Authorization Act, which forbade gender-affirming care for the children of military families—was signed by President Joe Biden.[11] Before I had finished it, an executive order banning *all* federally funded gender-affirming care for minors had been signed by President Donald Trump.[12] Given the rapidly accelerating pace and scope of all this legislation, I have no way of knowing how many more rights trans people will lose before this book reaches you.

Prior to the second Trump administration, healthcare bans primarily focused on youth transition, but they were never intended to end there. A *New York Times* article published in April 2023 reported: "Terry Schilling, the president of the American Principles Project, a right-wing advocacy group pushing for restrictions on transgender rights, said . . . that focusing on minors had been a short-term political calculation. His organization's long-term goal, he said, was to eliminate transition care altogether."[13] After Ohio passed one of the most restrictive youth healthcare bans in the nation, leaked audio from X Spaces revealed Republican politicians from Ohio and Michigan strategizing on how to ban gender-affirming care across the board.

"In terms of endgame, why are we allowing these practices for anyone? If we are going to stop this for anyone under 18, why not apply it for anyone over 18?" asked Rep. Josh Schriver of Michigan.

"That's a very smart thought there," responded Ohio Rep. Gary Click, who sponsored Ohio's youth care ban. "I think what we know legislatively is we have to take small bites."[14]

Here's something else that's known to take small bites: piranhas. Take enough of them, fast enough, and you reduce the bitten creature to its bones. What is all this, if it is not the violent assertion of patriarchal control over other people's bodies—the assertion that a trans body belongs, not to the trans person in question, but to "mankind," or "society," or the government, or simply to the people in power?

If feminism, which has been so clear and so brilliant on the ways cis women are denied bodily sovereignty, can't account for all these other patriarchal invasions, can it really be called feminism at all?

———

NO ONE IS more familiar with the ways that the patriarchy controls and delimits gender than trans people. My fear in the

Planned Parenthood waiting room—that some outside authority would deem me insufficiently manly and cut me off from further treatment—was not unfounded. It was, in fact, how transition historically works.

For most of the twentieth century, gender-affirming care was only available to trans people who passed a long battery of tests intended to determine their "true" identities, and the only sufficiently "true" identity was a stereotypical one. In a typical process, a trans person would need to see a psychiatrist for at least a few months, to determine if they were "really" transgender. They would then have to live in their preferred gender for up to two years, *without* hormones or surgery, thus dramatically increasing their risk of encountering transphobic violence and discrimination. Finally, if a clinician determined the "real-life test" to have been successful—and if the trans person hadn't been killed or impoverished over the course of the test—the patient would be granted a psychiatrist's letter giving them clearance for medical treatment, in the form of hormone replacement therapy (commonly, and understandably, shortened to HRT) and/or surgery. Some endocrinologists or surgeons required more than one letter before they would give care.

The goal was to screen out everyone except the trans people who could pass as "normal," stereotypical, non-trans members of their gender; the reward for passing all of these tests without being murdered was that you were expected to cut off all your friends and family members, move to a new location where nobody knew you, change your name, and live in hiding for the rest of your life, without disclosing your trans identity to anyone. Every trans person was a secret, known only to themselves, because we could not organize or demand rights if we were each the only trans person in the world.

I would have been denied care under this model. Most trans people would. I'm nonbinary and used "they" pronouns when I started HRT; nonbinary genders are not recognized by this system. Even if I edit my gender down to "man" (as I did when getting a therapist's letter for top surgery) I am married to another man; heterosexuality is part of "normal" masculinity, and openly gay trans men were only allowed to transition due to the advocacy and activism of Lou Sullivan, who became the first to do it in 1979. I had a relatively feminine presentation before coming out—I took ballet as a kid, played with dolls, etc.—so I can't claim irrepressible machismo, nor can I claim to have "always known" my gender. I sometimes bottom during sex; it's none of your business, but it would be my doctor's business, and they would ask me about it in order to determine my identity. Real men penetrate. They do not get penetrated. Once again, I'm out.

Now: Are there cisgender men who are attracted to men, who present in ways deemed feminine, who take ballet classes, who like being penetrated? Of course there are. You cannot rule me out of manhood without also ruling out Pete Buttigieg, Lil Nas X, Mads Mikkelsen (professional ballet dancer for eight years! Graduated from a top Swedish ballet academy! Look it up!) and many of the cisgender men I've dated. But you are not supposed to want to *be* those men. Under the standard of manhood applied to trans guys, even noted cisgender man, Bond villain, and all-around cinematic tough guy Mads Mikkelsen (his wife is his former choreographer!) doesn't measure up.

Trans women were typically placed under even crueler scrutiny, with doctors frequently refusing to clear their patients for transition unless they were attracted to them. Serano surfaces testimony from a member of the American Psychological Association who openly said, in 1974, that "he was more convinced of the femaleness of a female-to-male transsexual if she was particularly beautiful and was capable of evoking in him the same feelings that beautiful women generally do." Sexologist Ray Blanchard created an entire typology of trans women—real, "homosexual transsexuals" who were attracted to men and stuck to traditional female gender roles, and "autogynephiles," who supposedly fetishized the idea of being female—based on which women he found attractive. "Most homosexual transsexuals are much better looking than most autogynephilic transsexuals,"[15] wrote J. Michael Bailey, explicitly making hotness a criterion for being real.

It wasn't just looks. In her 2021 book *The Transgender Issue*, journalist Shon Faye tells the story of Dr. John Randell, who worked at the UK's first gender identity clinic, and treated "the vast majority of British people who medically transitioned between 1960 and 1980." Given his position of disproportionate authority, "woman" in those years meant whatever Dr. John Randell wanted it to mean. He could rule out anyone who didn't fit his criteria: For example, women "who would not consider taking up a more feminine profession after transition[.]"[16]

Now: I think a lot of men would like to force ambitious women out of their professions, or pass laws forbidding women to leave the house unless they're regulation hotties. The feminist movement exists to protect women from such abuses. Yet men who want to control what a woman can be are both allowed and encouraged to take it all out on trans women, simply because trans women have been forced to ask permission to be who they are.

Cis people accuse trans people of confusing gender stereotypes with gender identities, but this is projection. The people who do this are cis people who refuse to recognize trans people's gender identities unless we conform to the stereotypes they like. When trans people have reshaped the model of gender-affirming care, it has typically been to broaden the range of acceptable gender expressions. Trans people's demands—like informed-consent care, in which anyone can be prescribed hormones if they are informed in advance of the risks and side effects; this is the model currently practiced by Planned Parenthood—recognize that gender stereotypes pose a threat to trans well-being.

In this way, trans people have often done the work of expanding gender for cis people. Lou Sullivan, for instance, didn't just have to prove that gay trans men deserved medical care. He also had to prove that "man," as a category, was not defined by the sexual domination of women. Loosening the restrictive gender norms that oppress trans people means loosening them for everybody else, too.

———

TO HAVE YOUR relationship to your own body governed by someone who does not and never will share your needs, to have your most intimate decisions subject to that person's often-bigoted idea of what your gender should look like or be like: This, by now, should sound intensely familiar. So let us change focus, for a moment, to the other medical procedures that have been banned and regulated in this way.

In *The Story of Jane*, a history of the underground feminist collective that provided safe surgical abortions before Roe v. Wade, Laura Kaplan writes that the organization's founder, "Jenny," was suffering from Hodgkin's disease when she got pregnant. Jenny's doctors knew that carrying the pregnancy to term would kill her and petitioned the hospital board for the right to perform an emergency abortion. They were denied. Jenny's death was not enough of a foregone conclusion, and so she was required to get letters of permission from two separate psychiatrists, testifying that her unwanted pregnancy had made her suicidal, before surgery was allowed.

Abortion was illegal, and you can make the argument that the high bar for entry was caused by the bans. Yet in that period, it was not uncommon for doctors to deny women reproductive healthcare, not because it was illegal, but simply because their reproductive lives didn't fit the doctor's picture of womanhood. In another story collected by Kaplan, a woman asked her doctor for birth control shortly before her wedding. The pill was legal, but her doctor refused her anyway. "He told her to come back after the honeymoon," Kaplan writes.

Within living memory, abortion and birth control have been subject to the exact same gatekeeping measures as transition, with the same deadly results. For this reason, male medical control of women's bodies became a primary focus of second-wave feminism. "Through that whole experience, there wasn't one woman involved," Jenny told Kaplan, decades later. "It was men—the doctors, the hospital board—controlling my reproductive rights and condemning me to death." One of the major goals of feminism's second wave was to ensure that women (at least, the cis ones) had authority over their own healthcare. They believed that women were entitled to know how their bodies worked, and how to care for them, and to make choices based on their own needs rather than some paternalistic authority's idea of how they ought to be living.

The concept of bodily autonomy, as we know it today, arose out of second-wave feminism's protests of the male-dominated medical system. There were people who argued that abortion ought to be legal for the purpose of "population control," and others who argued that it was a health measure that could limit the number of people with disabilities—both arguments flatly eugenicist and rooted in the idea that doctors could and should control other people's pregnancies for the good of society. It was only feminists who argued that the *actual pregnant person* should be the sole arbiter of whether an abortion was right or necessary. In 1965, California abortion activist Pat McGinnis proclaimed for the first time that "a woman's body is her own and she has a right to it."[17] It's a principle that has guided the movement ever since.

Yet, if you can provide a convincing case for birth control or abortion, you can also make the full case for transition. Living in the wrong gender is a bodily invasion at least as painful as pregnancy, and its physical and emotional effects are just as long-lasting. Pregnancy is frequently fatal, but so is failure to access transition care—the rate of suicidality among trans youth, in particular, is terrifyingly high. Many of us believe that it is particularly unjust to deny a minor an abortion, because they are not old enough to handle pregnancy and parenthood without being traumatized; young trans people are particularly traumatized by going through cis puberty, and have only a limited amount of time to seek out puberty blockers before those changes start to take place. Finally, obviously, there is the fact that someone's gender is *not your business*, any more than their sex life or their number of children is, and that it is not a physician's or government's job to decide who is morally deserving of care.

Everyone's body is their own. Everyone deserves choices. Abortion and transition are both controversial and frequently banned because they are life-saving forms of healthcare that allow people to transgress their society's gender norms. Which brings me to my final point: Transmasculine people are sitting smack in the center of this Venn diagram. We are punished for being trans at the same time as we're punished for having genitals and reproductive capacity people associate with "womanhood."

How can someone be a man while also experiencing a form of oppression we almost always classify as a "woman's issue"? How can you treat a trans man "like a man"—which is, I believe, how most cisgender allies aspire to treat us—while also not denying the sexism or misogyny he may face? Gender as an identity doesn't give us a way to account for this, nor does gender as a language. To make this picture clear, we have to add a third dimension.

#3

GENDER AS
A SYSTEM OF POWER

("A MAN'S PLACE," "MEN'S RIGHTS,"
"WHO'S THE MAN IN THE RELATIONSHIP," ETC.)

GO BACK TO YOUR STICK FIGURES FROM EARLIER IN THE chapter. It's time to draw them again, but with a difference. Draw one male figure, one female figure, and one stick figure who is neither male nor female. Go ahead, I'll wait.

There. Did you catch it? Right there, at the third stick figure, you hit a wall—a planned gap in your imagination. You know the symbol for "man" and the symbol for "woman," but there is no universally recognized way to draw a person who is neither male nor female. The male stick figure is "universal," supposedly, but we know that he's also male—calling him neutral rests on the idea that Man is the default form of human and Woman is the Other. If you intended to draw a nonbinary figure, you had to make the symbol up—and this is true even (especially?) if you are a nonbinary person yourself.

If you were raised in North America in the twentieth or twenty-first century, you have been taught that there are only two genders, male and female. You have also been taught that one gender—the male one—is meant to rule over the other. You have been told that the differences between genders, including, but not limited to, their power differential, are "natural," innate, and "biological," and that they can be detected from birth, or even beforehand.

All of this is made up. It's not "natural," nor is it an accurate description of human biology. It's a political ideology—a *gender* ideology, in fact—that was created very recently by white European Christians and exported to the rest of the world through colonialism.

Feminists call this ideology "patriarchy" and it's a pyramid scheme: Men begin at the lower rungs, as absolute rulers of their wives and children, and slowly advance up the ladder by gaining power over other men. Men (cis men) assure their legacies by controlling the reproductive capacities of women (cis women)—the children are his, not hers, and he has to control nearly every aspect of her life to make sure this is the case. Patriarchy enforces a strict division between private and public spheres: Women (cis women) are responsible for domestic, sexual, and emotional labor at home, and men (cis men) occupy positions of power and influence out in the world. Men get paid for their public work. Women do not get paid for their private labor—it's something their gender is "naturally" designed to do.

This is not the only way humans can live. There are matrilineal and matrifocal societies. In *The Patriarchs*, a history of how patriarchal ideology spread across the world, science writer Angela Saini describes many of them. My favorite are the Mosuo of southwest China: "Mosuo children live in their mother's homes," Saini writes. "A man's place is in his own mother's home, helping to raise his sisters' children. Instead of marriage, when a young woman comes of age, she's given her own room in which to invite her lovers in the night, with the expectation that they will leave in the morning."[18]

So there you have it: Whether you are a dutiful housewife or a bachelorette entertaining a string of stay-at-home uncles depends, not on human nature, but on where and when you were born. Many cultures around the world also recognize more than two genders and/or the possibility of transitioning between them. What's more, these two factors—gender diversity and gender equality—reinforce each other. They do not conflict.

White Western feminism arises directly out of white women's encounters with those other cultures. The area where I live, upstate New York, is the birthplace of American women's suffrage. The reason for this is that it's the territory of the Haudenosaunee, an alliance of Native American nations who had a functioning democracy long before white settlers showed up. Haudenosaunee democracy, unlike the American kind, placed a strong focus on women's participation. Haudenosaunee women had the power to veto wars; they were responsible for electing male chiefs (and removing them for abuses of power—any man who committed sexual assault was ineligible for leadership); they conducted diplomatic negotiations and oversaw justice processes.

It wasn't just the Haudenosaunee. White settlers who encountered Native American communities were routinely shocked at the gender equality on display there. In early white America, wife-beating was legal, rape was an accepted part of the marital arrangement (and inflicted routinely on enslaved Black women), and there were still "public scold" laws that allowed men to exercise corporal punishment and public humiliation on women who were seen to be too opinionated or mouthy.

Native American men, on the other hand, seemingly did not rape women even when those women were enemies: "I have been in the midst of those roaring lions, and savage bears, that feared neither God, nor man, nor the devil, by night and day, alone and in company, sleeping all sorts together, and yet not one of them ever offered me the least abuse of unchastity to me, in word or action,"[19] wrote Mary Rowlandson, a white woman held as a prisoner of war by Narragansett and Wampanoag tribes in 1676.

White people described Native men's failure to sexually harass women as if it were something out of sci-fi, a mind-blowing scene from *Alien-vs.-Not-a-Sexual-Predator*: "I have seen young white women going unprotected about parts of the reservations in search of botanical specimens best found there and Indian men helping them," the missionary M. F. Trippe told a reporter. "Where else in the land can a girl be safe from insult from rude men whom she does not know?"[20]

This kind of thing could not remain a secret for long, and soon, white women began to demand the same rights and respect. Some, like early feminist Matilda Jocelyn Gage, lived with the Haudenosaunee in order to suss out how the "women's rights" concept worked, and how it could be best exported to the white community. The suffragettes were not spitballing or envisioning some never-before-seen utopia of female power—they were try-

ing to obtain power they had already seen exercised by Haudenosaunee women. White feminists knew a better world was possible because *they had been there*, even as they were responsible
for wiping it out.

Here's where it really gets interesting. Traditional Native
American societies also tended to have a high recognition of gender diversity and were far less likely to believe that gender was
derived from a person's body type. "The Yuma had a tradition of
gender designation based on dreams," writes Laguna Pueblo poet
Paula Gunn Allen. "A female who dreamed of weapons became a
male for all practical purposes." Elsewhere, among the Mohaves
and Cocopah, "gender-role designation was based on the choice of
companions and play objects of a young person. In such systems
a girl who chose to play with boys or with boys' objects such as a
bow and arrow became a male functionary."[21]

A world where children's gender is determined by their dreams,
by what they want, by what gives them joy: This, too, is and has
always been possible. It's important not to universalize or exoti-
cize here; we are talking about many societies, split across many
different times and places, not one monolithic Utopia. Still, this
history directly contradicts what the dominant culture teaches us
about the relationship between trans rights and feminism. Trans
existence has been routinely cast as a threat to women's equality or
safety—another Trump executive order, banning federal recognition of trans people's gender identities, was entitled "Defending
Women from Gender Ideology Extremism"[22]—and transphobes
have often held that embracing feminism or rejecting "gender
stereotypes" would make it unnecessary for anyone to transition.

Yet, in these societies, gender egalitarianism did not make gender diversity less common; it made it *more* so.

Here's Saini again, summing up the scholarly findings: "It may have been easier for people to cross genders in egalitarian Native American communities, because neither men nor women carried out jobs that were more highly valued than the other," she writes. "Without a difference in status, there were fewer barriers to negotiate."[23]

There it is: Transition is threatening to Western, Christian patriarchies because it entails a *change in status*. Bluntly, the only reason anyone cares what gender you are is that they need to know whether they can boss you around. Transition is scary because it introduces change into a supposedly inalterable hierarchy: Someone who was intended to rule throws her lot in with the rabble. A born underling dares to equate himself to his boss. In this system, the trans woman can only be a traitor, failing to uphold male supremacy; the trans man can only be a thief, claiming male dignity he does not deserve; nonbinary people can only be crazy, testifying to a many-gendered reality that does not and cannot exist.

Yet that reality *does* exist. It always has. The scariest thing about transition is that it forces us to realize that the gendered power hierarchies we live with are not "natural" or inevitable. If people realize this, they will want more, and if they want more, they will organize to get more, and if they get more, then the cis men in power lose every unfair advantage on which they've built their lives. The easiest thing to do is to eliminate trans and nonbinary people: Shoot the messenger and hope the message will go unheard.

Again: Many egalitarian or many-gendered societies are still around, very much including the Haudenosaunee, who have spent much of the past century suing the US government for the return of their traditional lands around Lake Onondaga. Still, globally, or in terms of the contemporary consciousness, patriarchy and its binary gender scheme dominate the narrative. It's so pervasive that many of us, including many feminists, assume it's the way things have always been. How did this happen? The short answer is "white people." The longer answer, which still amounts to "white people," is colonialism and the Catholic church.

We still don't know why European Christian culture became so heavily invested in patriarchy—it is partially, though probably not only, a matter of cultural inheritance from ancient Greece and Rome—but the historical record shows us that where white colonizers go, patriarchy follows. This does not happen solely through nebulous cultural influence, or even through propaganda spread by Christian missionaries (though both play a role) but through actual laws passed to prohibit egalitarian societal arrangements. In places where inheritance passed down through the female line, colonized subjects would be required by law to start willing their property to their sons. In places where women traditionally ruled, the colonizers would force them to hand their titles down to male heirs.

Whole civilizations had their histories rewritten to make patriarchy appear universal and inevitable. Yoruba scholar Oyèrónkẹ́ Oyěwùmí writes that Yoruba language is "gender-free"[24]—names, pronouns, and even titles (sibling, parent, spouse, etc.) are gender-neutral. Yet when English-speaking historians sat down to write Yoruba history, they interpreted the titles *oba* and *alaafin*—both of which mean, simply, "ruler" or "leader"—as "king." From there, they went on to teach colonized Yoruba subjects that their long lists of historical leaders were all men, despite Yoruba oral history saying otherwise.

As for gender diversity, well: Spanish conquistador Vasco Nunez de Balboa first encountered the Indigenous people of Quaraca in 1513, which is when, "upon discovering that some of the men 'dressed as women' and engaged in sexual relations with each other, he ordered forty of them to be thrown to his hunting dogs to be dismembered to their death."[25] Centuries later, Osh-Tisch, a leader of the Badé—Two-Spirit people of the Crow tribe who wore feminine clothing and referred to each other as "sister"—was continually plagued by agents from the Bureau of Indian Affairs, who repeatedly forced Osh-Tisch to wear male clothing over the protests of the community. When that didn't work, the BIA began seizing Osh-Tisch's sisters.

"The agent incarcerated the Badés, cut off their hair, made them wear men's clothing," says Crow elder Joe Medicine Crow. "He forced them to do manual labor, planting these trees that you see here on the BIA grounds. The people were so upset with this that Chief Pretty Eagle came into Crow agency and told the agent to leave the reservation. It was a tragedy, trying to change them."[26]

Patriarchy took over the world at gunpoint, suppressed or killed all evidence of life outside the binary, and then told us that it was "natural." Whiteness split gender diversity off from gender equality, then told us they were incompatible. Yet in very recent, very well-recorded history—history that is literally under my feet as I write this, and maybe under yours—we saw what society looked like without patriarchy, and we knew that Two-Spirit people were welcomed there. The patriarchal gender ideology has begun to chip and peel off, like a bad coat of paint, exposing the truth underneath it. The world we want is within reach, because it is the world we have lived in all along.

———

FEMINISTS HAVE TENDED to describe the white, Western Christian gender regime as "patriarchy." Queer and trans activists are likely to refer to it as the "gender binary." They're describing the same system from different angles: Feminism concentrates on patriarchy's defining power differential—male dominance and female oppression—whereas queer activism questions the belief in two immutable, mutually opposed genders upon which that hierarchy rests. While many cis people define "feminism" as the process of changing society so that cis women can be "equal" to cis men, transfeminists argue that as long as the process of sorting people into two distinct, opposed, "natural" genders goes unchallenged, inequality will always result.

These approaches are often framed as if they're opposed to each other—trans people supposedly constitute an existential threat to the "sex-based rights" of women, and feminists can't be trusted because they gave us the TERFs. Yet, in reality, they could not be more deeply interrelated. Someone with a uterus who controls their own reproductive capacity is flouting the patriarchal hierarchy—exercising control and ownership of their body, rather than letting "society" or the nearest cisgender man do the job—and so is the person who transitions. Sometimes, they're even the same person.

History tells us that gender equality and gender diversity are mutually reinforcing: Where you have one, it is easier to have the other. Common sense tells us the same thing. All denizens of patriarchy are continually surveilled to ensure they are "correctly" performing gender, and any deviations are punished. Thus, the proper aim of feminism is not to redistribute power within the existing system; it is to tear down that system and decouple gender from power once and for all.

This is the foundation of my feminism: Not cis women vs. cis men, or even women vs. patriarchy, but people of marginalized genders against the patriarchal binary, with the destruction of that patriarchal binary being the ultimate goal. I believe that our oppressions are so deeply intertwined that we cannot solve our problems without each other. I refuse to be pitted against any other gender-marginalized person on the path to my own liberation.

I am hoping you share this vision. (If not, it's pretty sad for you that you bought a book about it.) Yet defining "gender" is only the tiniest fraction of the work that needs to be done. We don't just need to describe our feminism; we need to live it. Let's take it out for a spin, then, and see how this particular feminism helps us live.

Part 2

SEX

A revolutionary in every bedroom
cannot fail to shake up the status quo.
—SHULAMITH FIRESTONE

THE THING ABOUT READING ABOUT YOURSELF ONLINE—
and, having done this for many years, I have had cause to realize
many horrible things about it—is that it gives you a false sense of
objectivity. In the early stages of my transition, I didn't know what
gender I was, or what names or pronouns I would wind up using,
or even what I looked like, but I always knew exactly what strangers were saying about me.

It is thanks to this diligent, tireless, and deeply unhealthy research that I knew exactly which question everyone would be asking when this book hit the stands—the one aspect of my transition that the internet has debated more often than any other. And, while I fully acknowledge that no sane, emotionally healthy person would read about themselves on the Reddit message board for Jesse Singal's podcast, I want that question to sound exactly as stupid as it is, so I'm going to quote the Reddit message board for Jesse Singal's podcast:

> "Jude has a husband, right? Does that guy have to pretend he's gay now?"

Here are the terms of our thought experiment: I'm still married to the same person I was before my transition. He dated and then married me believing me to be a woman; he remains married to me knowing that I'm a man. So: Is the sex we're having heterosexual? Homosexual? Was it straight before I transitioned, and gay afterward? Or was it gay the entire time, and if so, are all of my previous boyfriends retroactively bisexual?

In a better world, this would be a brainteaser or the riddle the Sphinx posed to Oedipus. (What is bisexual in high school, heterosexual in its twenties, and gay by middle age? Transgender Man.) In this world, it is a matter of pressing concern. My transition didn't just pose a threat to gender—it posed a threat to heterosexuality, and the ways men and women are supposed to relate to each other.

Of course, the ways men and women are supposed to relate to each other are pretty dismal. To explain, I need to tell you what sex was like when people thought of me as a girl.

———

THE SUMMER I turned nineteen, I went out with my friend's math professor. I ran into him at a local coffee shop. We wound up hanging out in a park, with a Hungarian friend of his, who had brought along a balalaika. I'm not sure anyone has ever enjoyed an impromptu amateur balalaika concert, but I guess I decided to find it continental. The guy was a professor, albeit my least favorite kind of professor, and he was a real grown-up, with a job and a car and his own roommate-free apartment, which made me feel special. I had watched *Manhattan* that semester, trying to feel more intellectual; I could easily see myself in the role of the wise-beyond-his-years younger confidante to some older man.

When he dropped me off at my place, he invited me to join him at a party later that evening, and I said yes. I went to the party. I drank two beers, maybe more like one and a half. I remember the number, because I thought about it a lot later on.

After the party, we went back to his apartment and made out. He put me up against a wall and reached for my underwear. I said no, and that I wasn't ready. We stopped. Then he started again. He reached into my underwear; I said no, and that it was only our first date. He stopped. He turned on the television. Then he started again.

Things went on like that for a while. I enjoyed kissing him, at least at first, and it felt rude to refuse—we were on a date, right? Kissing was expected—but I also knew I didn't want sex. I'd only had sex with two people, and both of them had at least claimed to love me. I'd just had my first real heartbreak that winter, and had been single for several months, trying to get over it. I didn't want my first new experience to be some after-party hookup with a guy I'd met that afternoon. I asked him to drive me home.

He pulled back, clearly irritated, and said that it was extremely inconvenient for him to drive me anywhere at this hour. It was dark. It was late. (It was maybe 10 p.m.) Couldn't I just stay at his place? I could, I said, but he wanted to have sex, and I wasn't going to do that. He was visibly angry by this point, contemptuous of me, and it stung. He told me that if I felt that way, I could sleep on the couch. Then he went upstairs to his bedroom.

There was no pillow on the couch, nor was there a blanket, and the apartment was freezing cold. It was summer, and the outfit I'd worn to the party was neither comfortable enough to sleep in nor substantial enough to warm me up under the blasting AC. He was mad at me, and I was anxious, a pull in the pit of my gut, like a kid being reprimanded by a teacher. He *was* a teacher. He was an adult man. He'd probably dated lots of people. I had dated two. Was there something wrong with me? Was I acting like a baby? Was refusing to have sex, asking to be driven home, actually rude or immature or cruel by adult standards?

I don't know what would have happened if I had fallen asleep. I didn't. I had let him leave the room angry at me, and I thought it was my job to make things right. I went upstairs, to his bedroom, and told him that I was cold. Maybe I thought he'd drive me home. Maybe I thought he'd turn nice again and regret losing his temper. He glared up at me, from his bed, and said: *Look, if you get into this bed, I'm going to fuck you.*

He did. I only remember bits of it. I know that I asked him to put on the condom. Asked and asked, and eventually got hit with another firm *no, I don't do that,* spoken in the tone of voice you'd use with a misbehaving dog. He flipped me around into different positions, trying to make it fun for himself. I assumed the poses he required. I was a fish on a hook.

What I remember most clearly is how badly my stomach hurt the whole time. It was a trapped, sour ache, the feeling of hope and excitement going bad. The other thing I remember, and cannot forget, is that it was still so fucking cold.

In the end, he hauled me into the shower and jerked off on me. I probably looked miserable. I didn't know which way to look, or whether he even knew I was there. I was ashamed, not for myself, but for him, somehow; his bowlegged chimp stance as he gripped his dick, the slack-jawed face he was making. My stomachache had gotten so bad that I thought I might vomit. I remember wondering how it could possibly be sexy to watch me standing still and looking sad and nauseous up against a tile wall. It was many years later when I realized that my misery might have been the turn-on. Given how the evening had proceeded, making me sad and sick could have been the point.

He took me home in the morning. I spent the rest of the day restlessly peregrinating between crowded places, different coffee shops and bookstores on my street, trying not to be alone. Then—

here's the really damning detail, the reason this case would never go to court—I called him and asked to hang out again. I thought if I could see him again, he would go back to being the nice guy I hung out with in the park. I thought that "one-night stands" were morally wrong, and that people who had them were bad and dirty; I thought that trying to date him would make me a good person and let me stop feeling used.

It didn't work. He drove me to a club, then left me at that club, while he took home a girl and did (the same thing to?) her. The next day, he explained that he wasn't interested in me. I tried to feel sad; I did feel angry. I told him that he hadn't used a condom, so he ought to pay for a pregnancy test.

Even all these years later, the demand for the pregnancy test makes me cringe. It was so clingy, so irrational, so stupid; I was so clearly acting like—*like a kid*, my forty-year-old parent-to-a-young-child's brain interjects, because that's what I was. The truth is that I knew I could not get pregnant from someone ejaculating in the same shower stall as me. I just needed some formal acknowledgment that he had hurt me. I was fixated on the condom, because that was what I had fought for hardest, and had been most forcefully denied. The pregnancy test was a way to name that damage. It was a way to say *you made me do something I didn't want to do*, and it was also a way to hold, in my hand, a little plastic piece of proof that I would be okay.

He brought the test over to my apartment, making sure to bring the Hungarian friend with him so that I knew he had plans and couldn't stay. I took it. It was negative. He drove off for another afternoon of casual misogyny and balalaika music. I called my mother and told her I wanted to come home. She picked me up and took me back to her house for dinner. I ate in my childhood dining room and slept in my childhood bed and, as odd as it seems, I don't think I cried.

The next time I saw the professor was over a year later. I was in a bar with a female friend—the same friend who had taken his class, actually—and he approached us through the crowd, smiling and purring my name and oozing what he thought was charm.

"Who's your friend?" he said, scanning her up and down with his eyes like a lecher in a silent film.

"She's not talking to you," I said.

His eyes narrowed, and I heard that other voice—the hard, mean, bad-dog voice he had used when denying me the condom.

"Oh, right," he said. "Because I'm *such* a *bad guy*."

Then he walked away.

———

THERE ARE TIMES when I have described the above encounter as sexual assault, or have been encouraged to describe it that way. There are other times when I'm not sure it qualifies. I have had experiences that are far less ambiguous: Once, at a local swimming pool, a group of boys surrounded me and pinned my arms behind my back while one of them thrust his hand up the crotch of my swimsuit. I'm not writing about those experiences. I'm writing about this one, because this specific type of encounter—the one that is normal, that is usual, that may even fit some heavily flawed definition of "consensual," but which still represents a degrading and dehumanizing use of another person built on a baked-in power imbalance—seems to be a ubiquitous part of heterosexual dating culture.

I saw it when the allegations against Aziz Ansari were published at babe dot net. ("It was 30 minutes of me getting up and moving and him following and sticking his fingers down my throat again," said the accuser, pseudonymously known as "Grace").[1] I saw it when my nineteenth-century literature class read *Tess of the d'Urbervilles*. ("For near three mortal months have you trifled with my feelings, eluded me, and snubbed me; and I won't stand it,"[2] the aristocrat Alec tells Tess, who wants him to stop touching her, before leading her into a dark woods where sex—somehow—ensues.) I see it every single time social media litigates the lyrics of "Baby, It's Cold Outside." ("'You're very pushy, you know' / 'I'd like to think of it as opportunistic,'"[3] goes one couplet.) In the archive of heterosexual interaction, what happened that night is supposed to happen, and does happen, over and over and over again.

Determining whether to call this encounter "rape" might matter, in some contexts. It would matter if I were to press charges. It would matter if I were to name him publicly, or report him to his workplace. I haven't done any of those things. No one has ever guessed who he is, based on my writing, and he has never contacted me to complain. In the course of writing this, I looked up his RateMyProfessor page. He is still teaching, at a different and better university, and (despite my feelings about giving him regular access to teenagers) he is getting pretty good reviews. The only real consequence this guy ever faced was being forbidden to hit on my friend at a bar. *He* clearly felt that was a bloodthirsty and draconian punishment, but in the grand scale of things, it hardly registers. Telling the story is something I do for myself, to give clarity to my own experiences. He—like the vast majority of guys who do this—is going to be just fine.

The truth is that we don't have to use the word "rape" in order to view this encounter as an abuse of power—a grown man exploiting a teenager's vulnerability and inexperience and desire to please in order to make that teenager submit to sexual acts they don't want or enjoy. We do not have to say that something is *illegal* in order to say that it is *wrong*; I shouldn't get prison time for spitting in your food, but you wouldn't want me as your waiter, either. Whether or not this guy broke the law—and I doubt he did, given that the laws of the era typically defined "rape" as the use of incontrovertible physical force—he was a scumbag. He hurt me. I know the pain is real, because I can feel it. That's got to be enough.

WHO GETS TO BE A VICTIM?
WHO GETS TO BE A GIRL?

"I do think even very supportive, trans affirming cis women feminists are often stopped by this idea that a trans woman, before coming out, cannot experience gendered violence directed toward women," says novelist and cultural critic Emily St. James.

One of my biggest worries about sharing my own story is that readers may use it to prop up a harmful narrative—one in which I can be accepted as a victim, because I was assigned female, but a transfeminine person can only ever be viewed as a potential threat.

St. James has lived through the other side of that dynamic. When she began writing about the abuse she experienced in childhood, she found that many self-declared feminists were unable to give her a real hearing. This was true even if they were nominally "trans-inclusive."

"You know, Hillary Clinton is a great example of a feminist who is nominally trans-affirming. Probably if I met her, she'd be like, 'Emily, hello.' You know, she's met Contrapoints. She's done the work," St. James says. "But still, I guarantee you that if I told her a story about my childhood and alluded to the fact that I was raised as a boy, she would overlay a set of beliefs about how I must have seen the world over that."

The assumption that St. James experienced her childhood as a "boy," or that she had a typically male upbringing, would wipe out much that is specifically trans about her experience—including the fact that she began telling people she was a girl when she was only three or four, and much of the abuse was intended as a punishment.

"What I experienced was horribly gendered," St. James says, "and horribly built atop a system of, 'Well, you think you're a girl. This is what happens to girls.'" Without that understanding, her feminist interlocutors "could understand someone abusing a child perceived as a boy, and be like, 'that was awful.' But there's this added layer in which it was a system of control designed to keep me from accessing who I was, a system of control designed to let me know my place in the social order."

Again: Patriarchy uses sexual violence and rape to patrol its borders—and trans people, as border-crossers, are always at high risk. Transmasculine people and transfeminine people experience sexual assault at around the same rate, which is even higher than the rates of violence against cis women. As per the US Office of Justice, at least 50 percent of us have experienced sexual violence, and that number may be as high as 66 percent, depending on which study you consult.[*] In the general population, 41.3 percent of all women have experienced "contact sexual violence," such as unwanted grabbing and grop-

---

[*] "Sexual Assault in the Transgender Community," Office for Victims of Crime, https://ovc.ojp.gov/sites/g/files/xyckuh226/files/pubs/forge/sexual_numbers.html#victims.

ing, and 21 percent have experienced rape or attempted rape.[†]

Every one of those victims has a story, and every story is important—but in order to understand the bigger picture, we need to hear each one on its own terms, without trying to wedge it into a preconceived narrative of what gendered violence or "violence against women" is supposed to be.

---

† "National Intimate Partner and Sexual Violence Survey," National Sexual Violence Resource Center, https://www.nsvrc.org/sites/default/files/2021-04/2015data-brief508.pdf.

No matter how long or hard I wrestle to define this encounter, the professor himself has probably never put any thought into it. He almost certainly remembers this as a standard, "consensual" hookup, if he remembers me at all. From his perspective, he was entitled to sex from the moment I entered his apartment, and he was licensed to do whatever it took to get it. This message had probably been drilled into him from the moment he hit puberty—his partner's pleasure, happiness, even basic safety were all less important than establishing himself as a successful Sex-Getter, because Men get Sex from Women, and that's what makes them Real Men.

I wasn't a person; I was a resource from which sex could be extracted. He was not my date; he was an invading army, and it was his job to win. It is not just that heterosexual culture is full of rape and violence against women—though it is—but that normal sex is also built on exploitation, misogyny, and gendered power imbalances an alarmingly large percentage of the time. Even when heterosexuality works the way it's "supposed" to, it works out badly for women.

Now: As it happens, there is a feminist with a pretty neat framework for this kind of thing. Buckle up, children; it's time to talk about Andrea Dworkin.

———

CITING DWORKIN IN a queer context is, to say the least, risky. After all, much of twentieth-century queer theory and activism arose specifically to repudiate her. There are people who will never forgive Andrea Dworkin: for her enmity toward the sex-radical queer feminists who were trans people's best allies; for her opposition to sex work, which trans people are exponentially more likely than cis people to do and be criminalized for doing; for her ties to the TERFs; for the anti-pornography ordinance she drafted with Catherine McKinnon, which provided the blueprint for countless right-wing "anti-pornography" offensives targeting queer people, including (for one very recent example) the Heritage Foundation's Project 2025, which threatens to classify all content about trans people as "pornographic," and to jail "pornographers"—meaning trans people and our allies—en masse.

For all this, and more, many trans people will never be able to trust Andrea Dworkin, or anyone who cites her, including me. I don't really think they're being unreasonable. I am not interested in valorizing any TERFs or whitewashing anybody's transphobia, and I will, I promise, dig into those objections in more depth later in this book.

WAS ANDREA DWORKIN QUEER?

If you've heard anything about Andrea Dworkin, you've probably heard that she was a lesbian. So: Was she queer? Not exactly. "Queer" and "lesbian," over the years, have been defined in many different ways, and one of the first things "queer" meant, in an activist context, was "specifically not Andrea Dworkin."

"Lesbian feminism," as it was defined in the 1970s and up through the '80s, didn't necessarily entail being sexually attracted to women. Lots of "political lesbians" were celibate. Others were partnered with men—Robin Morgan, for instance, was married to a man when she harassed trans feminist Beth Elliott out of the West Coast Lesbian Conference for not being lesbian enough.

To be a "lesbian," in this historical moment, signified that you were "female-identified," that you "reserved your energy" for women, that you lived for and within a female universe. It might also mean that you slept with women, but that was optional. In fact, overt sexuality was often frowned on as being patriarchal (as, for example, the harsh judgment of butch-femme couples for supposedly replicating heterosexuality, or the endless debates over whether lesbians should use dildos). Dworkin was a lesbian feminist in this sense of the term.

Queer and sex-positive feminism arose in direct opposition to this subculture. Queer feminism came from women who had been cast out or shamed by the lesbian-feminist zeitgeist: leather dykes, butch-femme couples, trans women, sex workers. It held that being a lesbian was, yes, about sexual attraction to women. It reclaimed toxic labels ("dyke" rather than lesbian, "fag" rather than gay, "queer" rather than anything in particular) and abhorred respectability politics. It held that queerness was about being a sexual outlaw, and treasured transgressive sexual expression—the obscene, the deviant, the pornographic—as a reservoir of resistance to heteronormativity.

Queer feminism, historically, has been vastly more accepting of (and more often led by) trans people than lesbian-feminism, which gave us TERFs. Part of my point, in writing this book, is that the two camps were not always at war with each other, and that we can learn something by looking back before the split. But this is why some people will always give me side-eye when I cite Andrea Dworkin: Not only was she not queer, we invented the term "queer" to describe all that she was not.

FOR NOW, I will just tell you that I read feminist theory like a cookbook. Its purpose is to teach you how to make something, in this case, a feminist life. Not every recipe in every cookbook will be appetizing. Some cookbooks are poorly written, some are too basic to be useful for a serious cook, some are intended for professionals and assume I have all sorts of specialized kitchen equipment that I never intend to purchase. Sometimes the cookbook is really old, and outdated, and you find a recipe for one of those hideous 1950s "salads" made out of strawberry Jell-O with corned beef and olives, or bananas wrapped in pickled herring. But even in a heavily flawed cookbook, you can often find a recipe that will nourish you. Maybe it's one recipe out of a hundred. Maybe that's enough.

Intercourse, published in 1987, is probably Dworkin's most famous book, and it contains at least one very useful recipe, which has been often misrepresented. *Intercourse* is popularly known as the book where Dworkin claims that "all sex is rape." That's not, however, what it says. What Dworkin wrote was that *intercourse*—not sex, not rape, but the very particular kind of penetrative sex men have with women when following the sexual scripts of patriarchy—was not about sexual expression or pleasure, but about the ritualized affirmation of men's social and physical dominance over women.

"The hatred of women is a source of sexual pleasure for men in its own right," Dworkin wrote. "Intercourse appears to be the expression of that contempt in pure form, in the form of a sexed hierarchy . . . Intercourse is the pure, sterile, formal expression of men's contempt for women."[4] The point of sex is not pleasure, or even the specific act of vaginal penetration, but reaffirming one's masculinity at the cost of some woman's pain or humiliation.

It all sounds pretty dire, but it does make a certain sense: If patriarchy is set up to ensure a power imbalance between men and women, but also to pressure them into heterosexual couples, then their sex will inevitably be informed by their power imbalance. If men are encouraged to hate women, and also to have sex with them, sex will be an expression of hatred at least some of the time.

This is an area where queer theory actually does back Dworkin up. In *The Tragedy of Heterosexuality*, queer feminist scholar Jane Ward writes that heterosexuality under patriarchy is built on a central paradox: "Modern notions of heterosexuality require men to feel love for women, the very population they have dominated and dehumanized for centuries." Men and women are supposed to wind up together, but men are not supposed to *like* the women they end up with, and—thanks to the patriarchal gender binary, which tells us that the genders are diametrically opposed, with no common ground or gray area between them—heterosexual partners are meant to have little or nothing in common.

Under these conditions, the idea that a sexual relationship between a man and a woman could be about love was hardly to be expected—and, for most of history, it wasn't. "Women were the people with whom men had procreative sex, and women of privilege (wealthy women, white women, women of high status) were sometimes perceived as delicate and virtuous, in need of men's protection and seduction," Ward writes. "But in none of these arrangements was 'liking' women, or regarding them as men's most logical and beloved companions, a requirement in the way that contemporary straight culture now presumes."

In fact, falling in love with a woman was "unmanly"[5]; it caused you to have a high opinion of her, to care about what she thought, and thus diminished your masculinity by putting a mere woman in a position of control over your life. Even the word "heterosexual" was originally the name of a mental illness—it denoted "a morbid sexual passion for one of the opposite sex,"[6] or, in other words, any interest in having sex with an opposite-gender partner for reasons other than procreation. Ask not for whom the DSM-IV tolls, cishets.

Sex, under these conditions, was about force and ownership, and marriage manuals mostly prepared women to endure it: "A certain pleasure in manifesting his power over a woman by inflicting pain upon her is an outcome and survival of the primitive process of courtship, and an almost or quite normal constituent of the sexual impulse of man," wrote sexologist Havelock Ellis, ultimately concluding that "what men are impelled to give, women love to receive," and that women would stop complaining once their husbands had pushed past the initial phase of resistance. Not all of them stopped. In 1918, marriage expert Mabel Stopes wrote about women who were "driven to suicide and insanity" by "the horror of the first night of marriage."

We generally do not expect the wedding night to be a gauntlet of sexual torture these days, but that history informs the present. To this day, what Ward calls the "heterosexual repair industry"[7]— the rolling circus of dating experts and books with titles like *Men are from Mars, Women are from Venus* or *Act Like a Lady, Think Like a Man*, or *He's Just Not That Into You*—teaches women tricks for managing male partners who are presumed to be hostile, unknowable, and fundamentally just not able to express affection in terms those women can understand. In the realm of pop psychology, sitcom jokes, and fabric softener commercials, heterosexuality still operates on the assumption that men and women are natural enemies, and that they've got to shack up with each other anyway, because that's just how life works.

Now: I'm not sure *every* single instance of sex between a man and a woman is an attempt to shore up male supremacy. Neither, for that matter, was Andrea Dworkin; her longest-lasting partnership was with a man, John Stoltenberg. Though Stoltenberg identified as gay and Dworkin identified as a lesbian and neither one identified as monogamous, they did—as per Stoltenberg and Dworkin's biographer, Martin Duberman—have sex with each other. They just didn't engage in vaginal penetration, because neither of them liked it.

So I am not—*not*—shaming women for being attracted to men, or partnering with men, and I am not blaming them for the abuse they may experience. Nor am I saying that all sex between men and women is violent. Nor am I saying that queer relationships are inherently safe or free from abuse. But, with all these potential misreadings cleared out of the way, what I *am* saying is that heterosexuality, the institution, is structurally violent—set up to produce violence, not as a rare tragedy, but as a regular and expected outcome.

What am I so frightened of when I tell the story about the professor? I worry that someone will tell me that what I described is *normal*, that it's nothing to complain about, that things like that happen all the time, and that as a grown man, I should be tough enough or worldly enough not to let it hurt my feelings.

But if that's true—if "normal" sex is something people with more power inflict on people with less, if a "normal" hookup frequently endangers the physical and psychological health of at least one person involved, if all our systems are set up to facilitate rape rather than discourage it—then is that not, itself, an outrage? Is that not an injustice worth protesting? Saying that something is wrong is not the same as saying that it is illegal—but calling something *normal* is never the same as calling it *good*.

———

JUST AS THE patriarchal gender binary sorts the world into men and women, and places one gender at the top of the world and the other beneath it, the heterosexual script sorts people into two roles: Done-To and Doers. The Doers stick their body parts into other people, which is tough, and active, and honorable, and masculine; the Done-To get things stuck into them, which is weak, and passive, and feminine, and gross.

Sex consists of sticking the superior partner's body part into the inferior partner's body part, thereby confirming the Doer's awesomeness and the Done-To's inferiority. Do that often enough, for long enough, and you might spend the rest of your lives together. Hooray.

These ideas also dog queer people: We, too, have our stereotypes about decisive, confident tops and dithery, people-pleasing bottoms. Queer people are brought up in the same patriarchy as straight people, and we carry it with us unless we make a conscious effort to put it down.

Still, for heterosexual masculinity, these stereotypes are more than just powerful—they are *constitutive*. To be a man is to fuck women, to fuck women is to penetrate women, to penetrate women is to dominate women—and the man who gets dominated, gets penetrated, or gets fucked has failed at his gender.

Which is to say, though the patriarchal binary tends to portray these roles as "natural," derived from the shapes of our genitalia, they are really political. In the terms set forth by patriarchy, a woman is someone who gets sexually used by a man, and someone who is sexually used by a man is therefore a woman. A man who does not use women sexually might as well not be a man at all.

This is what French feminist Monique Wittig was referring to when she wrote that "lesbians are not women"; not that lesbians don't identify as women (I'm told it's pretty common) but that "[the word] 'woman' has meaning only in heterosexual systems of thought and heterosexual economic systems."[8] Heterosexuality is baked into our binary gender system, as the presumed social and sexual norm that governs cross-gender interactions, so if you subtract it from the equation, what you are left with is not quite a traditional binary gender. It's something else.

You can also date or have sex with men, as a woman, without identifying as someone who exists to be sexually used by men. I hope you do. But women who attempt to have equitable cross-gender relationships are also bumping up against the constraints of the gender binary—and, like queer people of all genders, they are likely to be coerced, shamed, or assaulted for their noncompliance.

Men, meanwhile, are taught that their identity depends on being able to sexually conquer and subordinate women. To be subordinated to a woman—or even equal to her—robs them of their manhood, and so does sleeping with or being attracted to men. In fact, even letting your fellow men suspect that you might be gay negates your membership in the man club, and thereby all the power and privilege you get from being a member of the ruling class within patriarchy. The only way to regain that power is to prove that you can dominate someone from the lower classes—men are encouraged to lash out with violence at women and queer people, even or *especially* if they find them attractive, in order to preserve their identities as men in a patriarchal world.

AND THEN THERE ARE CHASERS

Trans women and transfeminine people are often subject to heteromasculine grodiness in even more intense ways than cis women. To wit: The archetypal figure of The Chaser, a straight man who fetishizes trans femmes yet fears them as symbols of his own possible queerness.

In their book *Gender/Fucking*, Florence Ashley discusses The Chaser in grim and witty detail: The guy who began a first date by showing them an iPhone video of a male friend "blowing three straight guys in an alley" to demonstrate his sexual open-mindedness, the dudes who retweet Ashley's fully clothed selfies "alongside swathes of pornographic videos and photos, under the panoptic gaze of their erection-*cum*-profile picture,"* or upload the same selfies onto porn sites, under the impression that Ashley's mere visible existence is a fetish.

Chaserdom, it turns out, is often indistinguishable from garden-variety straight-guy grossness, an unsolicited dick pic turned up to eleven. Yes, Ashley tells me, chasers reduce transfeminine people to their bodies: "But then the question becomes, is that actually any different from non-chaser men? Because hegemonic sexuality and gender norms

---

* *Gender/Fucking*, Florence Ashley, p. 27–28.

are themselves fundamentally articulated around this idea of male sexuality as objectifying women," they say. "The degrading elements of chasers, where they act like transfeminine people are objects and not full persons, is in many ways fundamentally just how male sexuality is structured in our society."

The difference, with chasers, is that they feel their straightness is being called into question. Some get off on it, which is weird and dehumanizing (the attitude is not "I'm proud to say my girlfriend's trans," but "I am a minority because that makes me kind of gay," as Ashley puts it) and some fear it, which is dangerous. It is not at all uncommon for chasers to turn violent and harm or even kill trans girlfriends to restore their own perceived heteromasculinity.

But that, too, is nothing out of the ordinary: "That also still sounds like just 'men,' right?" Ashley says. "Like, you know, the love of straight men lives dangerously close to violence." The point, here, is not that all men are innately terrible, but that treating transfeminine and cis feminine experiences as fundamentally different causes us to miss the bigger picture: "When we separate it, we only pay attention to the parts that are different in ways that maybe don't shed as much light on the total phenomenon as it could."

———

SO WE COME to the specific sexual crisis of the queer trans man: Why is it so scary when the female-looking partner in a "heterosexual" relationship says that they are not, and never have been, a woman? Without the status that comes from dominating a woman—sexually, socially, politically—how can the cis partner's masculinity remain intact?

"It's perceived as an act of unmanning," says Jay Edidin. "It's someone who is assigned female, and whom they perceive or choose to continue to label as female, actively taking what they see as masculinity or maleness. It means that it's not as elite a club as they thought it was, and it means, specifically, that the group of people [masculinity] was designed to keep out have access to it."

Edidin came out while cohosting a comics podcast with his then-husband, Miles Stokes—*Jay and Miles X-Plain the X-Men*—that had over fifteen thousand regular listeners. Unsurprisingly, a lot of those listeners had vocal opinions on his transition—and many of them believed it was an assault or an insult inflicted on his saintly cis husband.

"I'd Google the show and names associated with it periodically," Edidin tells me, "and I stumbled across a Reddit thread which very quickly turned into a conversation about my transition and what I was 'doing' to Miles, and speculating on the state of my genitalia."

On some level, the scrutiny and shaming was just an extension of what he'd always received as a female-presenting person in a public role:

"I mean, we've gotten comments from the start about what a bitch I am and how much it sucks that Miles is stuck with me; it made sense that transition added to that specific narrative."

Still, it's striking how neatly the sexist "bitch wife" narrative can pivot into a transphobic "trans widower" one. Even when I was only a public feminist, people made snide comments about me emasculating my husband. First, I was keeping his balls in a vice made out of used IUDs and old Marge Piercy novels; now, he's not even the only one with balls. The link, Edidin says, is "fear of female—because I think these men overwhelmingly still see, or choose to identify, us as female—power to subvert and undercut men's sexuality, and by extension traditional masculinity."

In a patriarchy, saying that my relationship contains two men is the same as saying it contains two *people*, where really it is only supposed to contain one person—the Man—and that handy home appliance, the Wife, who fulfills all his domestic and sexual needs. If I am a human being deserving of respect and dignity— which is what "man" means in gender-as-power-structure—then my partner can't be one. Only one of us can win the Man contest, because heterosexuality teaches us that every relationship has to contain a Done-To and a Doer, a superior and an inferior, a man and a woman: Someone who is held up, and someone who is kept down.

Of course: Taunting my husband about his masculinity or his sexual identity is also an invitation for him to prove it. The idea that he was "accidentally" attracted to a man or a trans person is supposedly humiliating for him, and in order to regain his manhood, he's got to exercise violent dominance over somebody, preferably me.

For me, this has been confined to rude internet comments. For other trans people, this is what gets them killed: Gwen Araujo, beaten to death with a shovel because the boys she was dating were afraid of anyone knowing they'd been with a trans girl. Brandon Teena, raped and then shot and then stabbed to death, because some straight bros found out one of "their" women was dating a trans man. Thirty-three states still allow people who murder their trans partners to invoke the "trans panic" defense—that is, to claim that they did not know their sexual partner was trans, and that, upon finding out, they were so horrified that they had no choice but to kill them. When people attempt to rile up my husband by asking if I turned him queer, they think they can get him to dump me, disavow me, or beat me up so that he doesn't look like a faggot. They want to press the button that makes him kill me.

I am lucky—very lucky—that my husband does not seem to have such a button. I can tell you that I wouldn't have married him if he were a bigot, but the fact is, I had no way of knowing how he would react to my coming out. Gender transition brings out unexpectedly ugly sides of cis partners all the time. Among trans guys who date or have dated men, the figure of the terrible first husband—the cis guy who beat or raped or psychologically and verbally tortured them at the least sign of gender nonconformity, all so that nobody would call him gay—is ubiquitous. The same statistics that tell us trans people are disproportionately subject to sexual violence also say that up to 50 percent of trans people have been hit by a partner after coming out.[9] There's no difference between me and those other guys, nothing I did or said that earned me a better outcome. I just happened to be fortunate in who I married. That's all.

Yet it would be a huge mistake to try to silo this problem—to call it a gay problem, or a trans problem, or a gay trans man's problem—without seeing all the ways this problem is bound up in misogyny, or patriarchy, or the rigged and self-defeating game of heteronormative relationships. The homophobia and transphobia I receive are inevitably bound up in the notion that sexual relationships are *meant* to be unequal, that women are meant to serve men sexually, that sex itself is primarily an act of conquest that exists to cement men's social and political domination of women. Until all those things change, my situation cannot change; I will be seen as a scary, emasculating monster, a worst-case-scenario, a "woman" gone horribly wrong, until the day when actual women can have equal and safe relationships with whomever they please.

To fix heterosexuality, you have to end patriarchy; to end patriarchy, you have to fix heterosexuality. They move in tandem, always together, and so does everyone who falls outside of *cis*, outside of *het*, outside of *man*, into the mixed bag we've labeled *queer*.

The truth is that I've never actually asked my husband if he's gay. I never set him down in front of the ever-expanding LG-BTQIA+ acronym and told him to pick a letter; I was too busy figuring out my own. My husband lost the protection of heterosexuality on the day a bunch of internet strangers started mocking him for marrying a man, and we both know it. I can tell you that he has never protested that loss, nor has he ever objected to a single step of my transition—nothing that brought me closer to visible manhood took me further away from him, and that's what matters. Labeling a relationship "gay" or "straight" matters less than what happens inside it and what we create through it: A world where people can love each other, and still be seen as human, and still be free.

Part 3

MOTHERS

*It is a radical act to nurture the lives
of those who are not supposed to exist.*
—LORETTA J. ROSS

WHAT ARE YOUR ASSOCIATIONS WITH FEMINISM? I ASK
Audrey, and on the other side of the Zoom call, Audrey pauses.
She looks away, looks back. She asks me to confirm I will only be
using her first name, and I confirm it. As it happens, her first name
isn't "Audrey"; given how much of her interview I've included here,
I'm using a pseudonym at her request.

So: *What are your associations with feminism?* I ask, and Audrey pauses again.

"My mother," she says.

Audrey's mother has a doctorate in women's studies, which she earned in the late 1980s and early '90s, from a school known for its liberal politics and strong queer culture. She teaches at a nearby university. She has studied under some of the leading lights of the second wave. Audrey can remember her mother leading her through museums of natural history, when she was a small child, explaining the ancient origins of patriarchy.

When Audrey came out as a trans woman, in her early twenties, she tells me, her mother took her out for ice cream.

"I had come out to her, but I couldn't start hormones until I started a new job, couldn't get the insurance for them, and was in that weird middle time," Audrey says. "And she took me out when I was home." There, over the table, Audrey's feminist mother looked her newfound daughter in the eye, "and was, like, 'so, can you explain to me why you don't think that the rights of transsexuals are in conflict with the rights of women?'"

Audrey's mother had strong opinions on transsexuals. She'd always had them; one Thanksgiving was ruined by the news that some women's colleges admitted trans women. "She was getting in a huge fight with my relatives because she was like, 'trans women have no place there,'" Audrey says.

Audrey still had a place in her own family, but it was becoming a painful one: "It's never 'I hate trans people, trans people should die,'" Audrey tells me. "It's only ever like 'I just have some *concerns*, but come over. I can make your favorite for dinner, but can we talk about my *concerns* for a second?'" Those concerns inevitably turned out to be transphobia, couched in the language of second-wave feminism: "It was largely stuff like, 'well, you know you can never *really* be a woman, right? You know that surgery is mutilation, right?'" Audrey says. "And then that turned into, 'well, I just feel like these rights are in conflict with women's rights,' or 'well, you're going to stay out of women's spaces, right?'"

"I consider myself a feminist, and I consider myself a feminist in the sense that I want to read more feminist thinkers. I want to actually become a more committed, more rigorous, thinking feminist," Audrey says. She deals with the same hassles as any other woman—objectification, discrimination, street harassment—and would like to ground her resistance in feminist politics: "A lot of my experiences in my life, particularly post-transition, are very in line with, 'yeah, this is fucking patriarchy,' and I want to have the language to talk about that."

Audrey pauses. She looks away, looks back.

"But it just feels like that world is poisoned, too," she says. "Because I know what happened with my mom."

———

I WANT TO tell you that feminism and trans rights have always been interconnected and inseparable. I want to tell you that there's never been any real conflict; that TERFs are a fringe sect, with no real connection to the mainstream movement, and that any intelligent or progressive feminist reviles them. I want to say that the mistrust and hurt many trans people feel toward feminism has all been one big misunderstanding, and that once I clear it up, we can all get together and drink wine and read *Les*

Guérillères and *Nevada* aloud to each other in our living rooms and laugh, and laugh, and laugh.

I want to say all of that, but I can't, because it isn't true. For some people, "feminism" is the reason they can't call their mothers when their hearts are broken. For some people, "feminism" is how their families and loved ones taught them to hate themselves.

It feels important to start here, with the story of Audrey's mother, because she isn't some fringe bigot who got radicalized on the internet. She isn't a religious conservative. She isn't a right-wing Moms-for-Liberty type who needs Chaya Raichik or Donald Trump to tell her who to hate. She's something much sadder: She's a nice, polite, respectable, well-educated, liberal feminist who is ashamed of her daughter for being a girl.

The politics of transness have become increasingly inseparable from the politics of childhood and motherhood in recent years; the concerned, "gender-critical" mother trying to save her child from transition is a ubiquitous figure in anti-trans organizing and propaganda. Some feminists cast trans people's very existence as an attack on women's sacred role as mothers, or on the "sex-based rights" that supposedly arise from childbearing.

This would have been repellent to the founding intellectuals of second-wave feminism. That feminism intended to trouble our ideas of gender as "natural," rather than cement them; it never wanted to put "motherhood" on a pedestal, or imply that it was women's destiny to do it, and it never said that "family" was supposed to only look one way. In fact, family—the traditional nuclear arrangement, with Dad as boss, kids as property, and Mom as the exploited worker hovering in between them—was one of the great obstacles to liberation.

———

HALF OF THE stories you've heard about second-wave feminism are stories about Shulamith Firestone. She founded the underground newsletter *Notes From the First Year*, which popularized consciousness-raising and published essays like "The Myth of the Vaginal Orgasm." She cofounded Redstockings (with Ellen Willis) and founded the New York Radical Women, the first radical feminist group in New York City. She organized the first abortion speak-out in the United States. She was among the first to insist that feminist women organize in their own right, rather than as auxiliaries of male-run groups. When the feminist movement had its decisive break with the student left—the Nixon Counter-Inauguration, where feminist women scheduled to deliver speeches were booed and terrorized off stage by men screaming "take her off the stage and fuck her!"— Shulamith Firestone was one of the women who got shouted off the stage.

Firestone learned about patriarchy where most of us do—at home, from her parents. She was born to a conservative Orthodox Jewish family; her father was a strict believer that men and women had preordained roles handed down from God, and he was determined to make Firestone fit her role. When she asked him why she had to make her brother's bed, his answer was "because you're a girl." They clashed throughout her childhood, and the clashes were often violent. As per Susan Faludi's 2013 profile of Firestone—to date, the closest anyone has gotten to writing a real biography—"her surviving brothers and sisters recall seeing Shulie and her father 'grappling' on the stairs of their family home; the elder Firestone shouted, 'I'll kill you,' to which Shulie shouted back 'I'll kill you *first!*'"

Firestone emerged into adulthood as a brilliant, pissed-off, chronically defiant young woman, determined to speak her mind, change the world, and never do anyone else's chores again. (In one infamous incident, when she was asked to help clean up a feminist meeting space, her reply—"I'm an intellectual. I don't sweep floors"—infuriated the other women present, who were apparently expected to keep on sweeping.) She was mercurial, difficult, arrogant, unstoppable; she was kicked out of every group she founded. In one confrontation, which goes to show that cis feminists could deploy claims of "male socialization" even against each other, a comrade alleged that Shulamith's ambition and assertiveness proved that she had "male hormones." Firestone pointed to her breasts and said, "But look at these!" It did not go over well.

Shulie was impossible. Shulie was irreplaceable. Shulie was active in the feminist movement for only three years, before it disowned her, in which time she more or less drew the map for the entire thing. Firestone, or the groups she founded, "occupied restaurants that wouldn't serve 'unescorted' women; conducted a 'Burial of Traditional Womanhood,' in Arlington National Cemetery (the deceased wore curlers); released dozens of white mice to wreak havoc at a bridal fair at Madison

Square Garden; held an 'ogle-in' on Wall Street, to dole out some payback to leering men; and, most notorious, hurled brassieres, high heels, pots and pans, copies of *Playboy*, and other 'instruments of female torture' into a Freedom Trash Can at the Miss America pageant in Atlantic City."[1]

Shulamith Firestone wrote only one book of feminist theory in her lifetime—*The Dialectic of Sex*, published in 1970—and the world is still, frankly, trying to catch up. It started where she started: With the rule of fathers.

"The term family was first used by the Romans to denote a social unit the head of which ruled over wife, children and slaves," she writes in *Dialectic*. "Under Roman law he was invested with rights of life and death over them all; *famulus* means domestic slave, and *familia* is the total number of slaves belonging to one man."

Firestone identifies the nuclear family as the basic unit of patriarchy. The father's absolute rule over wife and children provides the model for the male king's rule over his subjects, the male CEO's rule over his workers, the male priest's rule over his congregation, and the male God's rule over the world. For this problem, Firestone proposed a fairly drastic solution: The nuclear family, and motherhood itself, must be abolished.

"Pregnancy is barbaric," Firestone wrote. If pregnancy and childbirth were at the root of patriarchy, and if those processes were a threat to one's life, health, and happiness— "childbirth *hurts*. And it isn't good for you," Firestone noted, correct on both counts—then feminist liberation depended on finding some way around them. Assistive reproductive technologies, like artificial wombs, would allow children to be raised in large group settings, by many caring adults rather than one full-time homemaker and one all-but-absent dad. This would lift the burden of reproductive and domestic labor off women and allow for true gender equality. In the place of "the reproduction of the species by one sex for the benefit of both," we would have a world where "children would be born to both sexes equally, or independently of either, however one chooses to look at it."

In the early 1970s, Firestone's suggestions ranged from impractical to flat-out bonkers. That's why it's so useful to reread *The Dialectic of Sex* now, in the 2020s, and find that most of Firestone's wildest predictions are now commonplace parts of daily life. (In one passage, Firestone off-handedly suggests that schoolwork will get easier when humanity gets around to inventing Wikipedia: "After all, why store facts in one's head when computer banks could supply more comprehensive information instantaneously?")[2] From a contemporary vantage point, Firestone looks, not "eccentric," but *prescient*—and the future she predicted was queer.

We don't have artificial wombs (*yet*,—in September of 2023, *MIT Technology Review* reported that multiple companies are testing synthetic uteri on lambs and piglets in advance of human trials).[3] However, we do have a wide range of assistive reproductive technologies, from artificial insemination and in vitro fertilization to egg and sperm freezing for pre-operative trans folks, that are disproportionately beneficial to queer parents. Those technologies are not fairly distributed—they're hugely expensive, meaning that it's mostly white, middle-, or upper-class queers with health insurance who can get them—but for those who do access them, it is possible to create a child without procreative, penis-in-vagina sex.

Not coincidentally, those very technologies are routinely cast as monstrous, unnatural, or dystopian by conservatives. As I write this, Republicans are moving to ban in vitro fertilization; IVF procedures typically create more embryos than clients can carry to term, and an Alabama court ruling has found that "frozen embryos can be considered children under state law," and that the destruction of unused embryos is therefore abortion or the "wrongful death of a minor child."[4] A November 2023 feature in *Christianity Today* called frozen IVF embryos "the new orphan crisis" and "the next pro-life frontier," calling on evangelicals to adopt these embryos and carry them to term themselves, lest they be "abandoned."[5]

Anti-trans feminists are also devoutly opposed to these technologies. Julie Bindel calls surrogacy—the practice of carrying and delivering a fetus on someone else's behalf, either for money or as a personal arrangement—an "abomination" and "the pimping of pregnancy."[6] In 1979, Janice Raymond published *The Transsexual Empire*; by 1993, she had moved on to *Women as Wombs*, which argued that IVF and surrogacy were attacks on women's rights.

To be clear, there are legitimate feminist critiques to be made of the surrogacy business, and I have made them—the industry, in its current form, mainly consists of wealthy, white, Western families outsourcing the pain and danger of childbirth to third-world women of color. The argument that surrogacy is "unnatural"— a quality it shares with abortion, birth control, vaccines, indoor plumbing, and cooked food—is not feminist critique. Defining women around their sacred and fore-ordained role as mothers is sexism, plain and simple, and this is true no matter how much hazy *Mists of Avalon* moon-goddess rhetoric you manage to drape over the argument's patriarchal bones.

Firestone abhorred what she called "matriarchalist theory in the women's movement."[7] She believed that it glorified oppression by implying that women's subjugation had made them better people. She had no problem rejecting the idea that childbirth was central to "women's" rights, or to the definition of "womanhood"; in fact, she thought the entire category of "woman" needed serious revision.

The goal of feminism, Shulamith Firestone wrote, was not to elevate women over men, or even to put women and men on an equal footing. It was to destroy the binary gender system itself. A true feminist revolution would affect "not just the elimination of male privilege but of the sex distinction itself: genital differences between human beings would no longer matter culturally."[8]

Which is to say: At the very beginning of second-wave feminism, there is a clear and coherent rationale for rejecting biology as the sole determinant of gender, and for rejecting binary gender altogether. That critique rests on a rejection of the inherent rightness or naturalness of nuclear families—a position since taken up by many other feminists, from second-wave psychologist Dorothy Dinnerstein to the more recent works on family abolition published by Sophie Lewis and M. E. O'Brien.

Firestone's work is primarily remembered, these days, as an attack on compulsory motherhood—the idea that everyone with a uterus should be made to bear and raise children. The second wave's critique of the nuclear family did, in fact, lay the groundwork for abortion rights, for cohabitation without marriage, for childfree and single women to remain single and childfree as long as they liked. Yet that was only half of its intended purpose. The feminist rejection of the nuclear family was also meant to free *children*—the only people even more powerless than women—from their parents' tyranny, and the violence inflicted on them in the name of producing nice, normal boys and girls.

———

ABUSING AND SHAMING children has never been a feminist tenet. It has, however, been a core tenet of the white, Western, Christian gender binary, and it has been exported—like the rest of that binary—by settler colonialists intent on teaching colonized people the "right" way of doing gender.

In her landmark work *Caliban and the Witch*, Silvia Federici spotlights the Jesuit missionaries' work to convert the Canadian Naskapi. The Jesuits struggled to make the Naskapi believe monogamy and keeping women at home mattered, since, in a community devoted to the collective welfare of its children, an adult didn't have to be biologically related to a child to raise them: "You French people love only your children; but we love all the children of our tribe," one Naskapi man explained.

Thus, it was love for the children that had to be demolished in order to conquer the people. "The Jesuits' greatest victory . . . was persuading the Naskapi to beat their children, believing that the 'savages' excessive fondness for their offspring was the major obstacle to their Christianization," Federici writes. The first such beating was inflicted on a little girl. It was done publicly, so that all the Naskapi could witness "the first punishment by beating [that] we inflict on anyone of our Nation."[9]

Once you start beating the children, the transition to patriarchy is already underway. The radical feminist critique of the (white) (Christian) (middle-class) nuclear family has always been that it is the indoctrination center where patriarchal values are taught. It's not just that the power of CEOs and kings and Popes mirrors the power that fathers are expected to wield over their families. Those larger structures—capitalism, countries, churches—are modeled on the family. They are based on hierarchy, oppression, and violence because our earliest and most intimate relationships were hierarchical, violent, and unjust.

Childhood is where we learn how it feels to be small. It's where we learn what it means to lack power, and how we learn to crave it. Some children are taught that they can graduate out of powerlessness and become fathers. As adults, they may well wield their power more violently, and cling to it more anxiously, because they remember how awful powerlessness feels. Others are taught that powerlessness is their destiny; the best they can do is learn how to survive getting stepped on. Yet those children, too, have been taught to crave power and associate it with violence. When they grow to exercise some type of social power—mothers' power over children, white women's power over Black women, cis women's power over trans women—they may abuse those people in order to feel what it is like to be strong.

The nuclear family is also a factory for reproducing patriarchal gender—making children assigned female into little mothers, making children assigned male into little men. Yet the conditioning doesn't take perfectly every time. In some cases, it doesn't take at all. Queer and trans children—and feminist children, like little Shulie Firestone—disrupt the lines of transmission. They show that the roles we assign within families are not natural or inevitable. For this reason, there has been tremendous violence levied, over the years, to discipline, punish, and remold the genders of queer and trans kids.

In *Histories of the Transgender Child*, historian Jules Gill-Peterson writes that most of our medical technology for managing gender presentation comes from the experiments performed on intersex babies and children—large clitorises were amputated, small phalluses were "reconstructed" into clits, orifices were reshaped or created or moved, adrenal glands were cut down to size or taken out (an invasive process in which recovery was not assured; in at least one case, "the child was constantly sick, and the wounds became infected").[10] The children had no say in these procedures, or in which gender they would be forced to live in after the fact. For many survivors, the psychological damage was as bad or worse than the physical scarring.

It would be nice to tell you that this is all just history—the archives of Western medicine are, reliably, a bummer, unless you like hearing about leeches or people putting mercury in baby painkillers—but to this day, newborns with ambiguous-looking genitals are forcibly assigned a binary gender through surgery. In fact, this is where our language of gender "assignment" comes from. Queer children have always been, and are still, violently disciplined by the medical establishment: Twentieth-century "cures" for homosexuality included "testicular transplants, Metrazol-induced shock seizures, methyltestosterone treatments, various other castration methods including X-ray irradiation and oestradiol benzoate, CO_2 inhalation, and brain surgery,"[11] and most or all of these were attempted on children. A 2019 UCLA study found that "an estimated 698,000 LGBT adults in the US have received conversion therapy either from a licensed professional or a religious advisor or from both at some point in their lives, including about 350,000 LGBT adults who received conversion therapy as adolescents."[12]

The popular image of conversion therapy associates it mainly with cis gay or lesbian children, but trans children have always been caught up in it. In 2022, the UK newspaper *The Standard* profiled a trans woman named Carolyn Mercer. In 1965, when Mercer was seventeen years old, she told her vicar she struggled with feelings of being a girl; he sent her to a psychiatric hospital where she was strapped to a wooden chair and given electric shocks while viewing photographs of women. She has never stopped being trans, but today, at the age of seventy-four, she says, "I still have difficulty with feeling positive emotions."[13] Others may never be able to tell us their stories. In 1948, a trans woman living in Wisconsin asked to receive gender reassignment surgery. The state recommended that she be given a lobotomy instead.[14]

None of these interventions has ever made a child less queer, or less trans—but within patriarchal families, having an unruly child is worse than having a dead one. A mother who sent her trans child to Canadian conversion therapist Kenneth Zucker reported decades later that "her daughter was repulsed by the thought of a sex change but was still suffering—she'd become an alcoholic, and was cutting herself." She wanted to remold her child, to ensure the transmission of binary gender into the future. She ended up taking the future away altogether: "'I'd be surprised if she outlived me,' her mother said."[15]

RISKY PROCEDURES

It might initially be hard to see the connection between intersex children being *forced* to undergo genital reconstructive surgeries and trans children being *denied* the right to socially or medically transition. The link is bodily autonomy: Both decisions are based on a denial of the children's agency and the belief that they should be forced to live in whatever gender their adults have picked out.

Much has been made of the supposed "risks" of youth transition, or the experimental nature of the procedures. *The New York Times* has spent the past several years publishing dubiously sourced articles with titles like "The Battle Over Gender Therapy" ("More teenagers than ever are seeking transitions, but the medical community that treats them is deeply divided about why—and what to do to help them")[*] and "They Paused Puberty, But Is There a Cost?"[†]

Bluntly: We seem to have decided, as a society, that it's okay to perform genital and gender-related medicine on children, *unless* they actually want it. Children are already receiving gender-affirming medicine, and even surgery, but it has to be done without their knowledge, or against their will, in order to be okay.

"Circumcision kills more than a hundred babies a year in the U.S. alone," feminist scholar Cristan Williams tells me. "American parents want our babies' genitalia to adhere to our culture's gender stereotypes. And we're willing to risk that baby's life so that they undergo a gender confirmation surgery. And that is routine. That is not problematic."

---

[*] "The Battle Over Gender Therapy," Emily Bazelon, *The New York Times Magazine*, June 15, 2022, https://www.nytimes.com/2022/06/15/magazine/gender-therapy.html.

[†] "They Paused Puberty, But Is There a Cost?", Megan Twohey and Christina Jewett, *The New York Times*, November 14, 2022, https://www.nytimes.com/2022/11/14/health/puberty-blockers-transgender.html.

My first instinct was to scoff—there's no way that circumcision could be *that* dangerous, or I would have heard about it—but I looked it up. The precise figure is 117, and I found it in a *New York Times* article entitled "Benefits of Circumcision Are Said to Outweigh Risks."‡

As of this writing, no child has ever died from taking puberty blockers.

---

‡ "Benefits of Circumcision are Said to Outweigh Risks," Ron Caryn Rabin, *New York Times*, August 27, 2012.

———

THE FACT THAT discussions about child-rearing are automatically framed as discussions about *motherhood* is sexist. The institution of "motherhood," as we know it, is created largely by men's refusal to do the work of raising their children. Mothers get blamed for pretty much every adverse event in their children's lives, from autism to becoming a serial killer, while dads are applauded just for showing up. Dorothy Dinnerstein, in her famous book *The Mermaid and the Minotaur,* attributes misogyny to exactly this: Men have created a violent and unjust world, but mothers are responsible for making their children conform to it. Fathers are the source of the injustice, but they're never around, so they don't have to explain themselves. It's mothers—the parents we spend all our time with, the parents we trust, the parents who seem to love us—who leave us feeling betrayed.

Statistics on child abuse and maltreatment show that mothers and fathers are just about equally likely to abuse their children: In 2022, 48 percent of child maltreatment perpetrators were men and 51 percent were women.[16] Trans children are just as likely to be tormented or rejected by their fathers as they are by their mothers—consider, for just one well-known instance, the father of Luna Younger, who sued for custody of his then-seven-year-old trans daughter because his ex-wife was letting her wear long hair and dresses.

Yet the anti-trans movement—which is fundamentally conservative, and therefore sexist—has built a tremendous amount of its propaganda around the image of the concerned "mother," the woman who is forced to watch helplessly as the tides of gender ideology sweep her child away. The patronizing concern for "mothers" here is really just another appeal to the sacred patriarchal binary: Mothers are good women, women who've fulfilled their biologically decreed role, and as such, they are threatened by trans people, who reject those roles and erode them into meaninglessness.

So we need to talk motherhood, in order to understand the anti-trans movement—and we need to start by acknowledging that, yes, it really is harder than ever to be a mom. Motherhood is the number-one driver of the pay gap between men and women; women who never marry or have children earn nearly as much as men do, though men earn more whether they have children or not.[17] Women are more likely to drop out of the workforce or take part-time jobs when they have children, partly due to the fact that childcare costs more money than they could earn by working.[18] During the coronavirus pandemic, when childcare centers and schools shut down, women provided an average of 173 hours of unpaid child care, three times as many hours as men did;[19] men, meanwhile, believed that they were doing just as much parenting as women. (In one study, 45 percent of men said that they did "most" of the home-schooling during the pandemic. Only 3 percent of women agreed.)[20] According to one damning, oft-quoted statistic, single mothers report more sleep, more leisure time, and less housework than women with husbands.[21]

Bluntly: Under the sacred mantle of "motherhood," you find a lot of hard, unpaid, thankless work, and a family structure in which men exploit women's labor without even realizing how much work those women are doing. Feminism has always recognized the injustice of this and fought to change it. Socialist feminists like Federici organized around wages for housework, and worked to name all the feminized labor—domestic, reproductive, emotional, sexual—that is not accorded the same respect as "real" (male) work. In the second wave, staid liberal organizations like NOW organized to demand free, universal, twenty-four-hour-a-day childcare centers.

We still don't have free universal childcare, or any universal childcare, or even childcare that working-class families can comfortably afford. We still teach women that they shouldn't need help or remuneration to perpetuate the human species—women are taught that they will be incomplete without bearing children, that they "naturally" excel at raising them, and when the work of motherhood overwhelms them, we say, not that they were put in an impossible situation, but that they've failed at being women.

Into this void comes capitalism, which has never yet found a female insecurity that it cannot monetize. The parenting industry replaces sisterhood with self-improvement: Does being a mother suck? You don't need universal childcare—you need to work harder! Here's a lactation consultant. Here's a sleep consultant. Here's a teething consultant. Here's a still-having-sex-with-your-partner consultant. Here are fifteen different experts with fifteen different podcasts selling fifteen different $24.99 books to tell you how to stop being such a bad mom.

People are not meant to raise children in isolation. It's simply too much work. Historically, rearing children has always been a matter for extended families, and for communities. But in twenty-first-century America, where child-rearing is no longer a function of the community, it has become an individual hustle— something that you can perfect if you just read the right books, take the right classes, pay for the right toys and summer camps and private pre-K tuitions. The market "turned parenting into a branded identity, leading many to defend their own parenting styles more vehemently than ever before and creating a sense of obligation to 'do it right,'" writes Amanda Montei in her 2023 analysis of contemporary motherhood, *Touched Out*. Middle-class and professional white women, who had more disposable income, were particularly targeted by the self-improvement industry, and "felt particularly compelled to study up not only on how to have the best birth possible but also on how to produce the worthiest children, with the most advantages."[22]

What happens when you tell people to find their power in an inherently powerless situation? What happens when you make someone's sense of worth contingent on raising "ideal" children, given that children are human, and can only become themselves?

Well: One thing that happens is Mumsnet, a UK parenting forum that has become a central hub of anti-trans thought and activism around the world. In a 2021 article for *Lux Magazine,* Katie Baker did a deep dive of the forum's culture: "As I read thread after thread, I noticed that many of the posters wrote about feeling newly disenfranchised and isolated after giving birth for the first time; cast out of a society in which they had previously enjoyed power by virtue of their relative wealth and education," Baker wrote. These were "privileged women who had never felt marginalized until they gave birth and came to feel isolated in their nuclear households and (rightfully!) outraged at the lack of support for mothers in the U.K."

Rather than turning that anger toward capitalism or the patriarchy—or, God forbid, their husbands—these women concluded that the concept of motherhood was under attack by a society that failed to respect "female biology." For them, womanhood was defined, almost exclusively, by pregnancy and childbirth: "Being pregnant, giving birth and breastfeeding are the only time in my life that I felt a proper awareness that I am female," wrote one woman—and this awareness was accompanied by pride that "I have a female body and am doing something only a person with a female body can ever do."[23]

We are a very long way from Shulamith Firestone here: "The 'natural' is not necessarily a 'human' value," she wrote. "We can no longer justify the maintenance of a discriminatory sex class system on the grounds of its origins in nature."[24]

Again: Viewed generously (okay, *very* generously) these women are fumbling around in search of a political framework for their suffering. A more genuine feminism, one which stressed women's structural oppression, would lead toward structural solutions: Wages for housework, childcare centers, more flex time for working parents. (Or—again—there is the option of asking their husbands to do a single damn thing, in terms of raising their own children. It's not a big, sweeping, legislative solution, but Dorothy Dinnerstein might tell you that it helps.) It would encourage them to challenge the institutions and norms that produce unequal outcomes for women—including the patriarchal gender binary, which is, after all, responsible for the idea that women are "naturally" fit for a life of unceasing domestic toil.

These women don't have that framework. They have patriarchy, which tells them that "motherhood" is what defines a woman, and that women only exist to be mothers, and that "biology" is responsible for all of the above. They're clinging to an identity created and circumscribed by their oppressors, trying to find "power" in a role purposefully designed to be disempowering. Rather than questioning their assigned roles, they cling to them, trying to find some leverage or security; if they're not men, then at least they're not transgender. They may never be on top, but at least someone else will always be on the bottom. The quest for equality becomes a quest for an even more despised Other, some class of permanent inferiors onto whom they can direct their rage and feel—if only for the moment, if only conditionally, if only until their husband comes back into the room—as if they are in charge.

It's an ugly game, but it's an old game, and there are reasons that people play it—there really are rewards that certain women can reap by clinging to their patriarchally ascribed identities. (Katie Baker, for instance, produced trans-inclusive feminist coverage for independent outlets right up until she was hired by *The New York Times,* at which point her name began appearing on fear-mongering articles about youth transition.) We'll get there. First, though, we need to discuss what happens when these women have children with "female biology," and those children turn out not to be girls.

———

EARLY ANTI-TRANS PROPAGANDA rested on the idea that nearly all trans people were trans women: Janice Raymond, for instance, wrote that "85 percent [of 'transsexual surgeries'] are male to female," and that "the female-to-constructed-male transsexual is the token that saves face for the male 'transsexual empire.'"[25]

In recent years, however, trans boys and female-assigned non-binary people have become more visible, leading to headlines like *The Guardian*'s (literally) incendiary "'An Explosion': what is behind the rise in girls questioning their gender identity?"

"I might have seen one child with gender dysphoria once every two years when I started practising. It was very niche and rare," says one anonymous clinician interviewed for the article, but "now, somewhere between 10% and 20% of her caseload is made up of adolescents registered as female at birth who identify as non-binary or trans, with just an occasional male-registered teenager who identifies as trans."[26]

First, trans people were faking because there were no transmasculine people. Now, trans people are faking because there are *too many* transmasculine people. Take your pick. This is now the defining stereotype of transmasculine people, or maybe even of young trans people as a whole: Damaged, deluded "young girls" swept up in the fad of gender transition, who are in danger of destroying their beauty and fertility with testosterone, unless their parents step in to save them from making their own decisions.

The canon text for this wave of the panic is Abigail Shrier's *Irreversible Damage*, published in 2020. On the surface, *Irreversible Damage* is one more "what's wrong with our girls" book, along the lines of *Reviving Ophelia* (girls are too depressed!), *Queen Bees and*

Wannabees (girls are too mean!), and *Cinderella Ate My Daughter* (girls are too girly!). As the parent of a daughter, I can tell you that there are far fewer of these books when it comes to boys—we tend to assume that they Will Be Boys™ no matter what we do or don't do, whereas girls are evidently born clinging to the edge of the abyss with one tiny fist.

It's common for books in this genre to assume a sort of bland, middle-of-the-road feminism, and *Irreversible Damage* does this, speculating that teenage "girls" (that is, trans boys and nonbinary people assigned female) are transitioning because of internalized misogyny and negative body image and the media's unrealistic expectations of women and whatnot. The veneer of girl power is remarkably thin; reading the book closely reveals that Shrier does not much like girls, and she certainly doesn't like feminism. At one point, she speculates that "inflated collegiate sexual assault statistics [have] scared adolescent girls off womanhood entirely." In another chapter, she blames feminists for making girls "jealous" of men. Telling women they've been "made victims by a 'system' that, generation after generation, locks us out and shuts us in with so many glass ceilings and walls," she writes, is "an exhausting set of untruths."

Similarly, though Shrier sometimes claims (like many people) to believe that trans boys are self-loathing lesbians, and that transition is a form of conversion therapy aimed at rendering their attraction to women socially acceptable, she also blames parents of trans boys for being too accepting of lesbianism: "Many of the parents I spoke with told me that when their, say, thirteen-year-old announced she was lesbian, they immediately supported their daughter." This, evidently, is a mistake. "If you eliminate all conflict through endless agreement and support, it may only encourage her to kick things up a notch," Shrier writes, reasoning—not inaccurately!—that if you are horrible and cruel to your child the *first* time they come out, they probably won't trust you with a second round.

Underneath the chatty, just-us-moms tone, what is being recommended here is good old-fashioned child abuse. Cutting your kids off from the internet ("reintroduce privacy into the home") and forcibly isolating them from peers ("if she is still living with you, a move seems incredibly effective . . . if she is in college, bring her home") are just the first steps. Shrier's favorite case—one she recommends, repeatedly, as a model for how these things should be done—concerns a teen who was pulled out of school and sent to do hard labor on a farm with no internet access: "The physical labor helped her reconnect to her body, and the lack of internet allowed her to leave her trans identity behind," writes Shrier. If I ever need anyone to write a cheery brochure for a prison camp, I'll know who to call.

Some part of this worldview is simple misogyny: Shrier refers to youth transition, more than once, as a form of female "hysteria." Yet it goes deeper than that. For one thing, Shrier is not equally worried about all transitions: "I wonder . . . whether it is no coincidence that so many of these kids come from upper-middle-class white families, seeking cover in a minority identity?"[27] she writes, appending a question mark to a fairly declarative statement.

A transmasculine child is not just a threat to the patriarchal family; they are a threat to that family's whiteness. Now, finally, we can talk about the structure underlying all of these appeals to motherhood: Not gender, but race, and white parents' need to extend their own genetics into a future of unquestioned and unquestionable white rule.

———

THE GENDER STEREOTYPES we've inherited and learned to call "sexist"—women as gentle, weak, nurturing, emotional, sexually passive; men as competitive, strong, assertive, rational, sexually dominant—are intended, not just to describe gender differences, but to describe how gender works *within whiteness*.

"The idea that sex is dimorphic—that there are two types of sexed body, and that they're clearly delineated—has a racist history," writes gender historian Kit Heyam. "As nineteenth-century scientists developed racist taxonomies of human beings, grouping people into the racial categories we've inherited today, they also developed theories about sexual dimorphism." Namely, race scientists argued that "white people's bodies were the most 'perfectly' divided into male and female, while people of color had fewer differences between the sexes."[28]

All those nineteenth-century hoop skirts and corsets and fainting couches were intended, not just to restrict white women's freedom, but to emphasize their extreme physical and mental difference from white *men*, and hence men's supposed racial superiority. White women were encouraged to deploy traditional "femininity" as a social strategy; it gave them less power than white men, but it also consolidated their power over all non-white people, regardless of gender.

Gender equality and gender diversity, meanwhile, were bad precisely because they were associated with people and civilizations of color. Patriarchy was what made white people white. If you examine racist stereotypes, you will often find that they subtly or not-so-subtly rely on the Other doing gender wrong. Heyam points to the supposed "femininity" of Asian men, or the "masculine" strength attributed to Black women. Likewise, the hypersexuality projected onto Black and Latina cis women—like the hypersexuality often projected onto trans women—is meant to degender them, by accusing them of lacking the sexual timidity and reticence we attribute to "real" white women.

ONLY PEOPLE HAVE GENDERS

The dichotomy between "correctly" gendered white people and un-gendered people of color was particularly acute in American slavery. The scholar who is referenced in just about every discussion of the topic—including this one—is Hortense J. Spillers, whose 1987 essay "Mama's Baby, Papa's Maybe: An American Grammar Book" illuminated slavery itself as a violent degendering of Black people.

Black slaves, Spillers wrote, were the abstract and genderless "flesh" against which white people's humanity, femininity, and masculinity could become legible, the background that provided the contrast. Part of the process of slavery is to reduce a person to property, an object or a thing, and objects do not have gender. Slavery was *"a theft of the body,"* Spillers writes, and "under these conditions, we lose at least *gender* difference *in the* outcome, and the female and male body become a territory of cultural and political maneuver, not at all gender-related, gender-specific."* In white supremacist patriarchy, to recognize someone's gender is to recognize their humanity—and dehumanizing them wipes away their gender along with everything else.

---

* *Trans Studies Reader Remix*, ed. Susan Stryker and Dylan McCarthy Johnston, p. 95.

It's useful to know this for a few reasons: First, it tells us that whiteness requires misogyny and subordination of women in order to exist. Whiteness also requires the presumption that there are two distinct sexes, which are not just different, but opposites, and that it is morally wrong to blur the distinction between them. Stereotypes of women as fragile, weak, and passive are specifically meant to describe (and delimit) white femininity; biological essentialism in the matter of gender is meant to shore up a supposed "natural" hierarchy of race. If you try to fight the transphobia or the sexism without also fighting the racism that creates them both, you will fail, because you will never actually remove the root cause.

Secondly, this widens our definition of "gender nonconforming" in useful ways. Trans people are still a fairly tiny minority—in the US, we comprise 1.6 percent of adults, and around 5 percent of people under age 30[29]—but if you look at *everybody* who stands accused of doing gender wrong, that group historically includes everyone but white, cis, straight, stereotypically masculine men. (Women are always doing gender wrong, even when they buy into white womanhood, because they are non-men in a system where only ruling-class men are considered fully human.) Correct gender, like any other type of power, is kept in the hands of the few at the expense of the many—everyone else is stuck chasing an ideal they can never reach, an ideal that is, in most cases, purposefully built to exclude them. Not many people are trans, but the majority of people on this planet are gender nonconforming.

Finally, and most importantly, it keeps us mindful of intended outcomes: Gender is a tool for reproducing race, not the other way around. I mean "reproduction" here very literally. One of the defining features of a patriarchy is that property and inheritance pass along the male line—men consolidate power and wealth by handing it off to other men. Yet, in 1662 in Virginia, the law changed, to say that a child's status would be inherited from its *mother*.[30] This was not intended to damage patriarchy, but to shore up slavery: From then on, if a white man impregnated his white wife, their child would be an heir, and if he raped and impregnated an enslaved Black woman, their child would be another slave.

"The systematic, institutionalized denial of reproductive freedom has uniquely marked Black women's history in America,"[31] writes Dorothy Roberts, in *Killing the Black Body*. Black women and people assigned female have never had reproductive autonomy in the States, she writes, and long after the end of slavery, the white establishment has presumed a unique entitlement to interfere with and control Black pregnant people's lives.

Under slavery, the chief means of control was forced childbirth—white men raped Black women to enrich themselves with children they could sell or use as slaves. After slavery, white control largely took the form of eugenics and "population control," arguing that Black children (and their mothers) posed an undue burden on society by taking up too many resources, and that their numbers should be limited.

In the 1980s, Reagan targeted the social safety net by spreading propaganda about Black "welfare queens," even though most of the mothers on public assistance were white. In the 1990s, Black women were disproportionately pressured to go on long-acting birth control implants like Norplant and Depo-Provera; those medications had uniquely severe side effects, and in some cases, doctors refused to take the birth control out when women asked. Today, the reproductive technologies that are game-changing for white queers are out of reach for many people of color: "Black women in particular were about twice as likely as white women to experience infertility and about half as likely to use ARTs,"[32] writes reproductive historian Laura Briggs.

The pressure on Black women *not* to reproduce was the flip side of the demand for white women to get pregnant at all costs. In the 1960s and 1970s, wrote Loretta J. Ross and Rickie Solinger, "a white woman typically could not be sterilized unless her reproductive output satisfied a formula devised by the medical profession: her age multiplied by the number of children she had already given birth to had to equal 120 or greater." (By this metric, I would become eligible for a hysterectomy on my 120th birthday. How nice to have something to look forward to!) Significantly, the patient also "needed the approval of two doctors and a psychiatrist before sterilization was approved."[33] At the very same time, mass sterilizations were being carried out on Black people with uteruses—some as young as nine years old—without their consent. The procedure was so common that it was nicknamed the "Mississippi appendectomy."[34]

In order to be "the norm," white people have to be the numerical majority—it's hard to keep your boot on someone's neck when you're outnumbered. Even as state laws permitted nonconsensual sterilization of anyone deemed unimportant or problematic, leading government figures including Theodore Roosevelt "exhorted white Americans to avoid committing 'race suicide,' a calamity that would befall the country if white women did not reproduce often enough to maintain the demographic advantage of 'the race.'"[35]

Internet Nazis nowadays call it "white genocide," but the core concept is unchanged: White people with uteruses have a social obligation to get pregnant, and everyone else has an obligation *not* to. It's through this lens that we can finally address the loudest and most obnoxious discourse about transmasculine pregnancy: The specter of the delusional "teenage girl" who is "sterilizing herself" with a gender transition she will later come to regret.

First of all: Transition is not sterilization. Some trans men get hysterectomies, but not all of us do; testosterone usually makes one's period stop, but trans men have to use birth control no matter how long they've been on HRT. I do not think the people spreading these talking points will stop just because they're medically inaccurate—most talking points about trans people are—but, if you're a trans person who is interested in getting pregnant, or if you just aren't sure what birth control you need, I feel I should include the information.

That said, it's worth asking *which* "teenage girls" we're worried about. Pictures speak louder than words here, so let's look at the pictures.

- On the cover of *Irreversible Damage*, for example, the "daughter" is represented by an illustration of a little girl with a theatrically missing uterus. (In fact, her whole midsection appears to be missing.) The disemboweled girl is white.

- In reporter Jesse Singal's infamous 2018 cover story for *The Atlantic*, the teaser text—"Your child says she's trans. She wants hormones and surgery. She's 13"—was superimposed over the face of twenty-two-year-old model Mina Brewer. In 2020, Brewer, who is transmasculine, came forward to say that the editors of *The Atlantic* never warned him that he would be misgendered on their cover, nor had they told him what kind of article would accompany his picture.[36] That's one interesting fact, and here's another: Mina Brewer is white.

- In Laura Dodsworth's "The Detransitioners," a 2020 photo series of women who reportedly regret transitioning to male (this would be the same spread that provoked Dodsworth to voice her fear of living without a uterus), every woman is portrayed nude, against a glowing white background, as if going off testosterone has allowed her to transcend her earthly form and ascend to Heaven. Every single woman, as far as I can tell, is white.[37]

The fear here is not "missing uteruses," it's missing *white* uteruses. The "transgender craze" is just "race suicide" with a new hat on—a moral panic over the possibility that white people assigned female are somehow refusing to breed.

Once you leave respectable bookstores and newsstands for the wilds of the internet, this gets a lot less subtle. There, anti-trans thought has crossed streams with the wider world of white supremacy and conspiracy theory. Transition is framed as a sinister (and Jewish) plot to reduce the white birth rate or undermine white Western masculinity. Where Abigail Shrier drops hints about social justice–crazed teens, driven to betray their own whiteness by spending too much time on Tumblr, Alix Aharon, of the conspiracy theory blog Transgender Medical Scandal, says it straight out: "Black youth are not transitioning."[38]

In the current conversation, trans men are a threat because we are seen as reducing the number of available white uteruses, taking white babies off the table, and anyone with a uterus is just a tool for the reproduction of white patriarchy, useful or useless, depending on how they might help the men in power keep control of the world.

Some white cis women will cling to patriarchal models of womanhood and femininity, because they've calculated that the advantages they earn from white solidarity will be greater than those they lose by abandoning feminism. Some will convince themselves that clinging to white privilege is feminism, albeit a very individualistic you-go-girl ladder-climbing variety of the thing. But the whiteness of this conversation gets more glaring the longer you look at it: The mums of Mumsnet are defined, not just by their marginalization as mothers, but by the fact that—as upper-middle-class white women—they never encountered marginalization before having children. Abigail Shrier is not just out to save our girls, she is out to save white children from rejecting their own privilege.

Mothers who refuse to affirm their trans kids are not following the logic of feminism, but they are perfectly in tune with another, older logic of gender and power. The patriarchal gender binary is white, and maintaining it is a white project. So maybe, by stepping outside of white feminism, we can find real answers about what feminists owe our kids.

———

BELL HOOKS WAS a smart girl, and that was why her parents decided to break her. hooks was born Gloria Jean Watkins, one of seven children in a working-class Black family in rural Kentucky. hooks did not look like her father's side of the family, and when her father was beating her mother—which he did, sometimes— he would accuse her mother of cheating on him. She was always aware she might not be his child.

Most of the time, however, father and mother were united in grinding Gloria down. "She could hear him telling the mama that the girl had too much spirit, that she had to learn to mind, that that spirit had to be broken," hooks writes in her memoir, *Bone Black*, a book that floats dissociatively between third and first person as the memories of her abuse become more and less bearable. Teaching her to "mind," to stop speaking up for herself, was part of teaching her how to be a woman: "She was too smart, men did not like smart women, men did not like a woman whose head was always in a book. And even more importantly men did not like a woman who talked back."

hooks's parents told her that no one would love her, that she would die alone; they told her that, if she kept reading books, she would go crazy and be locked up in an asylum. Sometimes, they invited her siblings to be part of the mockery. In one of the more harrowing scenes in *Bone Black*, hooks's mother invites her sisters to mock her, too: "In the kitchen with my sisters, she talks on and on about how she cannot stand me, about how I will go crazy." hooks, driven to near hysteria, burns herself with a hot clothes iron to make them stop. Her sisters and mother laugh at her: "They do not stop talking. They say no one will visit me in the mental hospital,"[39] hooks recalls.

hooks, more than any other feminist, grew up to be uniquely attuned to the injustice and terror visited upon children. She saw them as an oppressed group in their own right, terrifyingly vulnerable to adult whims and without recourse to justice. In her book *All About Love*, hooks tells the story of a social gathering where "a young professional, the mother of a small boy, bragged about the fact that she did not hit, that when her son misbehaved she clamped down on his flesh, pinching him until he got the message." Shocked, hooks pointed out that "had we all been listening to a man tell us that every time his wife or girlfriend does something he does not like he just clamps down on her flesh, pinching her as hard as he can, everybody would have been appalled." The other people at the party brushed her right off: "Most call themselves good liberals, supportive of civil rights and feminism. But when it came to the rights of children they held a different standard,"[40] hooks wrote.

hooks was critical of calls for "abolition of the family," calling it "terribly threatening." hooks felt white feminists were too quick to assume that family was the whole problem and work was the whole solution—Black women had always had to work, from slavery onward, and that work had hardly liberated them. "Many black women find the family the least oppressive institution," she wrote, precisely because it was the one place where they were valued as something other than mere faceless laborers. "Despite sexism in the context of the family, we may experience dignity, self-worth, and a humanization that is not experienced in the outside world where we confront all forms of oppression."[41]

Yet hooks knew full well that the family was the primary indoctrination site for ideologies of patriarchy and male domination—and she was clear that both women and men carried out that indoctrination. (hooks called her own mother "the strongest patriarchal voice in my life.")[42] According to hooks, the problem was not men, nor was it women, nor was it family or sexism or any other obvious culprit; it was the fact that our culture ran on an ethos of domination, expressed by the supposed right of the powerful to control and punish those beneath them.

"While male supremacy encourages the use of abusive force to maintain male domination of women, it is the Western philosophical notion of hierarchical rule and coercive authority that is the root cause of violence against women, of adult violence against children, of all violence between those who dominate and those who are dominated," wrote hooks. When a mother pinched her son, or a queer woman abused her girlfriend, or hooks's mother and sisters threatened to institutionalize her for not behaving like a real woman, no adult men were present—but *patriarchy* was, in the form of the belief that relationships were inherently hierarchical and that power equaled violence plus control. "It is this belief system that is the foundation on which sexist ideology and other ideologies of group oppression are based," wrote hooks, and "they can be eliminated only when this foundation is eliminated."[43]

Electrocuting your queer child, or institutionalizing them, or rejecting them and leaving them homeless, or sending them off to a farm to shovel shit until they stop telling you they're transgender—assuming such total and appropriative control of a child that they are not free to choose their own future or their own body or their own name—is a glaringly clear example of that coercive authority at work.

The traditional nuclear family is built on domination, and it teaches us that all relationships are about domination—that "to love" always means to be either one up or one down in a violent hierarchy, the target of your superior's cruelty and the cause of your inferior's pain. Whether it's mothers or fathers or both dealing out the violence, there is little that is more purely patriarchal than the quest to dominate and discipline kids out of being trans.

hooks proposed to counter the false "love" of dominance politics with an ethos of real love. It sounds wishy-washy when you type it out—but this is not vague, pop-psych, New Age, "All You Need is Love" love. It has more in common with Buddhist concepts of *metta*, or loving-kindness, or with Martin Luther King Jr.'s love ethic, which saw justice as the practice of love in the public sphere. hooks's love was tough like a muscle, a verb, an ongoing practice; it was "the will to nurture our own and another's spiritual growth," and it required "care, commitment, knowledge, trust, responsibility and respect." It was incompatible with hierarchy, with force, with dominance, with dehumanization: "We cannot claim to love if we are hurtful and abusive. Love and abuse cannot coexist."

hooks was clear that, on those terms, her parents had never loved her, and they had probably never been loved themselves: "Had my parents been loved well by *their* parents they would have given that love to their children. They gave what they had been given—care." Yet you also cannot nurture someone's spiritual growth without acknowledging that they have growing to do. Love does not abuse, nor does it coddle the abusive or harmful behavior of the beloved. Loving a child means holding them up as irreplaceable and inherently worthy, while also seeing what they could be, and refusing to let them be any smaller than they are.

Finally, love has to be done in community. No one can love alone. hooks did not call to abolish the family, but she believed that responsibility for children ought to be spread outside of it, and that breaking down the culture of dominance required twisting the patriarchal family into queer new shapes. hooks was clear that her life had been saved by the adults outside of her immediate family—her grandmother Saru, or a woman at her family's church who praised her reading, or her gentle pacifist grandfather, Daddy Gus, who was mocked for not behaving like a real man just as often as she was ever mocked for not behaving like a woman—and as an adult, she tried to be a saving presence in the lives of other children.

In *All About Love*, she writes about serving as an unofficial co-parent to her friend's child. When there was a debate between daughter and mother—for instance, over whether the daughter was old enough to get an allowance—hooks came in to facilitate dialogue. "Love and respectful interaction between two adults exemplified for the daughter (who was told about the discussion) ways of problem solving," and "by revealing her willingness to accept criticism and her capacity to reflect on her behavior and change,"[44] the girl's mother showed her that authority and infallibility are not the same thing.

hooks was not alone here. Black feminism has a particularly rich history of arguing for mothering as a communal responsibility, from Patricia Hill Collins to Alexis Pauline Gumbs, from James Baldwin's assertion that "the children are always ours, every single one of them, all over the globe,"[45] to Lucille Clifton's reminder after the Columbine school shooting that "these too are your children, this too is your child."[46]

As hooks explained it, Black families had always been denied the *Father Knows Best* patriarchal structure, even as they were punished for not upholding it, and unlike wealthier white people, they couldn't simply purchase care on the open market. Thus,

Black people, and particularly Black women, had instituted practices of caring for each other: "Even in families where the mother stayed home, she could also rely on people in the community to help," hooks wrote. "She did not need to go with her children every time they walked to the playground because they would be watched by a number of people living near the playground. People who did not have children often took responsibility for child-rearing."[47] This tradition fostered community by bringing children into regular contact with their elders, who they might not have met otherwise, and it allowed people who were not biological parents, like hooks, to have children in their lives.

This is not the large-scale techno-commune that Firestone envisioned, but it's not the isolation and market dependency of the traditional nuclear family either. It is an attitude we can take now, today, from wherever we are standing—love as an act of political will, the sense that all of us are responsible for all of us, and especially for our children. We need that kind of love now, and we need it badly, because children are dying for the lack of it every day.

———

IN FEBRUARY 2024, while I was in the very early stages of writing this book, Nex Benedict died. It was the second high-profile murder of a trans teenager in as many years; almost exactly one year earlier, on February 11, 2023, a sixteen-year-old trans girl named Brianna Ghey had been stabbed to death by her classmates in a public park. It was also the second high-profile death of a transmasculine person: In November 2022, Daniel Aston, a twenty-eight-year-old bartender, had been shot to death in the attack on Club Q, a gay club targeted on the eve of the Trans Day of Remembrance, a holiday when trans people gather to remember those of us who have been killed over the past year.

Nex Benedict, like Brianna Ghey, was sixteen. Their school district was not kind to queer children; one student told reporters that they'd been forced to leave school and attend classes online because of violence, which the teachers refused to stop. Benedict had been bullied relentlessly for their transness, culminating in an event in the school bathroom, where some girls pinned Benedict down and beat their head into the floor until they lost consciousness. The school refused to call an ambulance. Leaked body camera footage from a school security officer showed Benedict in a hospital bed, while Sue Benedict, their mother, pleaded with the officer to tell her why no one was being disciplined, and what was being done to protect her child. The school security officer told Benedict's mother that Benedict had brought the attack on themselves by splashing one of the girls with water.

Twenty-four hours later, Nex Benedict was dead. The death was eventually ruled a suicide. I can only say that, for a suicide, Benedict seems to have received a whole lot of encouragement to die.

I am leaving you here, in this grim place, because this is the truth: Sue Benedict loved her trans kid. Her love radiates off the body camera footage, in her fury, in the strain and tremble of her voice, in her desperation to know that something will be done and that her child will be safe with someone when she is not present. Brianna Ghey's parents loved and affirmed her; they mourn her now. Daniel Aston's parents loved him, deeply, and they still do. A year after his death, they told reporters that they keep a memorial to him in the front hallway of their home, with his picture in the center of it, so that "we can say hi to him every morning."[48]

With all the love in the world, these parents still lost their children—because it avails parents very little to love their trans children if the world still hates them. We can teach individual cisgender parents to support and affirm their trans children, and we should do so, but as long as the world at large is still hostile to trans people's existence, their kids will die.

Whether or not we are parents, whether or not we have trans children at home, we have a responsibility to make the world safer for trans kids, to be part of the number (I honestly do believe it's a growing number) of adults rooting for them and looking out for them, ready to protect them when their parents can't be there. If we are queer or trans ourselves, that work takes on a special urgency—whether or not queer people have children, we have children, because there is a whole universe of queer and trans kids out there, and many of them are not getting proper care at home, from the adults who are supposed to provide it. Care for those children can be our most fundamental form of resistance; there can be trans people who have never hated themselves, never doubted themselves, never been alone or lonely, so long as we are there for them from the moment they show up.

What is being asked of us is so small and so all-important: To love all the children of our tribe, and not just our own children. To recognize that the children are always ours, our joint responsibility and our shared future, no matter who their parents may be. It's a love that is inseparable from justice, and it has the potential to heal everyone who gives it. Every trans adult was a trans child once; when we look out for today's children, we also give ourselves the world that we always deserved.

Part 4

MEN

*The male rebel is rebelling
against being male.*
—VALERIE SOLANAS

I USED TO KEEP A NOTEBOOK FROM MY NIGHTS WORKING
the phone sex line. I swore I would write about it someday, but by
the time it was over, I was embarrassed that I'd ever done it, and the
notebooks were lost in some move or other, and now, here we are.

I took the job doing phone sex the year I moved to New York.
I couldn't get a job waiting tables in Manhattan, because I wasn't
good-looking enough—I was Midwest cute, several degrees too
average to snag a customer-facing job in a town filled with mod-

els—and my live-in boyfriend, who had just graduated from college with a fine arts degree, had exactly as much income as all recent fine arts graduates, which is none.

I saw the ad in the back of the *Village Voice*, and it promised $15 an hour for a job you could do without being seen. I thought it was adventurous and funny, a big-city thing to do, and my boyfriend said it would probably give me something to write about. The few girls I knew who had done it seemed fine, or at least, I hoped they were. They were all fine arts graduates, so they were thankful for the work. I took the job. I took my notebook. It took about three months, in total, for the job to break me.

There were lots of rape fantasies. Lots of incest, typically daddy-daughter. Lots of adult men who wanted to trick or pressure very young girls into sex; legally, we were required to stipulate that the girls were eighteen, but in the fantasies, they acted much younger. One man told me in detail how he would rape me to death while he burned my tits until they bubbled and melted, then bash my ribs in until they poked up through the skin of my chest, and there was probably some other stuff, but the most salient detail is that immediately after he hung up, I got a call from a guy who wanted to celebrate his daughter's eighteenth birthday by raping her up the ass while she cried. I started crying for real, while he described it to me, and he just came that much quicker. He must have thought I was really great at my job.

I had to take all these calls, and I had to cooperate, because I wasn't allowed to hang up. On our first day, they told us that girls who hung up got fired. I had nightmares, after the snuff call, but the specific violence of any given fantasy wasn't really what got to me. It was not being able to say "no." It was having my hands tied behind my back, unable to fight or resist, while every guy who called me took a swing. Even the most vanilla calls were predicated on the assumption that I was a woman, and that I had a lot of sex, and that women, especially the ones who had sex, were evil and disgusting: I heard *bitch, slut, whore, cunt,* over and over, from every guy who called me, and it wasn't in a fun, sexy, role-playing way—it was the way you cuss out a waiter, or a bartender, the way you talk to someone when you know they can't talk back. One man told me he was a writer. I asked him who his favorite authors were; he laughed and said it was cute of me to pretend that I could read.

The longer I was on the line, the more I came to understand that my helplessness was the draw. The guys got off on degrading me, more so than sex—they'd call up fuming mad at their wives or their female bosses, some woman they couldn't yell at without consequences, and I would have to let them insult me and call me a cunt until they calmed down. I would listen to them describe how much they hated the women who loved them (their flabby asses, their saggy tits, their dry pussies, and they wouldn't even *try* anal) or how they secretly wanted to fuck their daughters (who were flaunting it, by the way, total sluts, little bitches, how old was she? Uhhhh . . . let's say eighteen). I'd have to giggle and coo and sympathize, and then, I'd have to jerk them off, so that they could feel like the world still operated the way it used to—like at least one woman was subservient to them, and therefore, they were still in control.

The anger built up and up in my gut, night after night after night, and there was nowhere for it to go. It felt like giving birth; there were these wrenching contractions of rage rippling through my whole body, while something huge worked its way toward the surface. After one particularly bad night, I stood in the break room at dawn looking out at the skyline and hoping the whole city of New York would fall into the sea. Later that day, while I was eating lunch in Queens, the East Coast fell into a massive power outage. For a second—sitting, dazed, in the restaurant, as my debit card failed to go through the suddenly lifeless register—I thought I had caused it. I thought my anger had taken on a life of its own and plunged half the country into the dark.

I started finding reasons to pick fights with men, ways to make them pay for paying for me. I bought a tiny Catholic schoolgirl skirt on St. Mark's Place, and wore it with an ancient, mostly transparent wife-beater and the gigantic tanker boots I got from the army surplus store, waiting for the wrong kind of guy to give me the wrong kind of look and make himself fair game for some feminism.

I'd noticed that men always expected women to move out of the way for them; no matter how obviously a woman was headed in their direction, they just stuck to their chosen course along the subway platform or the sidewalk, expecting women to graciously glide out of their path. It was a simple, silent, everyday act of domination, a tiny bit of the female deference they took for granted. So I'd lock eyes with a guy, and then I'd walk straight at him, waiting for him to notice where I was going and get out of my way. When he didn't, I'd lean in with my shoulder and bodycheck him, hard, sending him gasping and stumbling across the pavement.

Sometimes the men shouted at me. Sometimes they hit me, though never really hard; I guess they were being chivalrous. Some of the men did nothing when I plowed into them, just gaped at me with a lost, wounded look, like they couldn't understand why anyone would be so mean to them. *You deserve it*, I thought, smiling back at them. *All of you deserve it.*

Fucking men.

———

I HAVE BEEN accused of hating men as often as anyone. I have sometimes hated them: Their privilege, their violence, their blindness to other people's realities, their arrogance, their self-pity, their entitlement, the fact that even when they have everything handed to them, they still see themselves as victims, and they still want more.

I have attributed all of that to *men*, the whole accursed species, the same way you would attribute racism to *white people* or homophobia to *straight people*. I've done that even though I know that #NotAllMen do those things, and that many men don't experience the privilege of manhood undiluted. I have done all that, and not felt bad about it, because—to my way of thinking—if any man is evolved and feminist enough not to participate in the behavior I'm complaining about, he is also evolved and feminist enough not to police the way other people talk about sexism.

Then I realized that I was a man. Then I began participating in trans spaces. And then, to my great and sorrowful surprise, I realized that many, many trans people did not trust me, or want me around, because they saw me as a "man-hater." Some of them were jerks, or sexists, but most of them had simply been burned by feminist rhetoric about men and now shied away from it. Man-hating, they told me (when they bothered to talk to me) was transphobic. Trans women were attacked and excluded in the name of hating "men," even though they were never men. Trans men, hearing feminists talk about man-hating, learned to hate themselves.

My first instinct, when I heard this, was to get defensive. I felt that the pain and oppression I'd experienced were being dismissed, that I was being told to bury what had been done to me for the sake of someone else's comfort. I felt that some large part of feminism rested on the ability to name men as an oppressor class, and that my core values were being attacked. I felt, in other words, the same way I imagine some of you will feel reading this.

Transition often means questioning everything about yourself and your life. If you can't be sure what gender you are, then you can't be sure of anything else, either. It's profoundly scary, and yet it can also be useful; with no preconceptions and no certainties, you let the world in and learn more in a few months than you could in a lifetime of safety. If you've already transitioned, you know this, but if you haven't—and, frankly, I'm imagining that cis readers will be more likely to freak out about what I'm saying here—then maybe this can be your invitation to experiment with that kind of radical, scary openness.

Because: Even though it's true that "misandry," the idea that men receive some special persecution or oppression on the basis of their manhood, is completely made up, gender essentialism, or the belief that all "men" and all "women" share the same core traits, really does harm trans people—and essentialist beliefs about men can be just as harmful as stereotypical conceptions of women, in certain circumstances. Moreover: It really is true that some feminists confuse essentialism with radicalism, and cling to reductive stereotypes about men and women even when they are causing profound harm.

The patriarchal binary teaches us that there are two immutable genders, and that they're completely distinct from each other: Men are all inherently like this, and women are all inherently like that, and never the twain shall meet. The framework that Julia Serano calls "oppositional sexism" furthermore tells us that men and women are mutually constructed opposites, so that whatever a man is, a woman is not, and vice versa: Men are logical, so women are emotional. Men are dominant, so women are submissive. Men are strong, so women are weak. And so on.

It's easy for us, as feminists, to spot the problem with that line of thinking. However, when we try to do feminism without rejecting the binary and its logic, we can wind up importing essentialism and oppositional sexism without realizing it: Men are violent, so women are nonviolent. Men want sex and not love, so women want love and not sex. Men are predators, so women are trustworthy. Men are oppressors, so women are incapable of oppressing anyone.

In reality, each of us can probably name violent women, predatory or exploitative women, bigoted women, and even—gasp!— women who enjoy casual sex, but the pseudo-feminist binary wipes all that nuance out. Our thinking doesn't actually change, the polarity just flips, so that Woman becomes the preferred category.

Moreover, binary thinking still harms women and contributes to their oppression, even when we're doing it for "feminist" reasons: I don't think any woman on the planet actually benefits from the belief that she is *inherently* and *unchangeably* sexless and selfless and harmless and nurturing, even when these are presented as positive traits. Moreover, if you believe women are virtuous because they are the oppressed half of an oppressor/oppressed dynamic, you are—consciously or not—constructing an argument for women's continued oppression. If getting the shit end of the stick within patriarchy makes you a better person, then women would be worse people if their situation improved.

Different schools of feminism rationalize their gender essentialism differently. Biological essentialists will tell you that aggression and dominance and sexual violence are caused by testosterone and hardwired into men's brains and bodies. Other radical feminists will tell you that "man," as a category, is simply a name for the dominant position in patriarchy: A man is someone who oppresses women, and so if gendered oppression were to disappear, there would be no men, just as there would be no women to experience oppression.

Trans guys are not accounted for by either system. If manhood is defined by having naturally high testosterone levels or being born with a penis, then you can't define us as men—most of us are born with the same genitals as cis women, and many of us have gone through female puberty and lived with estrogen-dominant systems. If manhood is defined as occupying the dominant position within patriarchy, or not being subject to misogyny, then we're not men by that standard, either. When we look like women, we receive much the same treatment as women, and whether or not we transition, we remain gender-marginalized for our entire lives.

The only way to respect trans men as men, while also not ignoring the oppression we face, is to recognize that gender identity and gender as a system of power are two different things. A trans man can occupy the marginalized, feminized, "inferior" position in our patriarchal gender hierarchy while still being very much a dude. Unless you can hold those two realities in your mind at once, you can only ever see us as deluded or dishonest women who aspire to be oppressors. That does not generate a tremendous amount of empathy or solidarity, and it also happens to be untrue.

Here, though, is the problem with framing all this as a matter of "man-hating." It just sounds so fucking *whiny*. No matter how reasonable the dude's arguments are (and I flatter myself that I've been reasonable here), it always sounds like some man complaining that not everyone likes him or listens to him or takes him seriously, and that's incredibly easy to dismiss. Patriarchy is meant to benefit men as a gender, systemically, not to benefit each man individually, so a man who's failed to receive his full reward is hard to feel sorry for: *Go cry into a list of Fortune 500 CEOs, buddy. Somebody's getting all that male privilege.*

Yet I really do believe that gender essentialism in the feminist movement harms everyone, not just trans guys. (To be clear, even if it only harmed trans guys, you should care about it—you should care about trans guys, generally—but that's not the case.) So, before I break your heart with the tale of my oppression at the hands of the Misandrist Matriarchy, I would like to show you how this issue affects and harms people other than me; namely, women.

1

TRANS WOMEN

"JANICE RAYMOND'S *THE TRANSSEXUAL EMPIRE* IS CHAL-
lenging, rigorous, and pioneering." This is what Andrea Dworkin
wrote about *The Transsexual Empire*, in a rave that was printed
on its back cover. "Raymond scrutinizes the connections between
science, morality, and gender. She asks the hard questions and
her answers have an intellectual quality and ethical integrity so
rare, so important, that the reader wants to think, to enter into a
critical dialogue with the book."[1] This is the version of the blurb
quoted by Raymond, when she is insisting—as she often has—
that Dworkin agreed with her about trans people. The version I've
read is shorter and hovers in bold type on the front, just above the
book's title: "'Crucial reading.'—Andrea Dworkin."

Now, finally, we can talk about why so many trans people har-
bor a deep distrust of the second wave. The movement began as
trans-inclusive, or at least, trans-agnostic. By the late 1970s and
early 1980s, it had adopted transmisogyny as a central part of its
platform, and even feminists who had once affirmed trans people—including, but not limited to, Dworkin—were complicit in
the shift.

Early in her career, Dworkin wrote, strongly and unambiguously, in support of trans people: "Every transsexual is entitled to
a sex-change operation, and it should be provided by the community as one of its functions. This is an emergency measure for an

emergency condition,"[2] she wrote in her first book, *Woman Hating*. She was adamant that "humans are a multi-sexed species," and that biological sex existed on a continuum rather than a binary: "It is not true that there are two sexes which are discrete and opposite, which are polar, which unite naturally and self-evidently into a harmonious whole."[3]

In those early works, Dworkin believed that feminism could and should eliminate transphobia: "By changing our premises about men and women . . . the social situation of transsexuals will be transformed, and transsexuals will be integrated into community, no longer persecuted and despised."[4] Even the Raymond blurb is more complicated than it looks. Though Raymond insists that Dworkin agreed with her, in the actual correspondence that's been published, Dworkin seems to have been telling Raymond to lay off.

> I knew of transsexuals in Europe as a small, vigorously
> persecuted minority, without any recourse to civil
> or political protection. They lived in absolute exile,
> as far as I could see, conjuring up for me the deepest
> reaches of Jewish experience. They were driven by
> their ostracization to prostitution, drugs, and suicide,
> conjuring up for me the deepest reaches of female
> experience. Their sense of gender dislocatedness was
> congruent with mine, in that my rage at the cultural
> and so-called biological definitions of womanhood
> were absolute . . . Male-to-female transsexuals were in

rebellion against the phallus and so was I. Female-to-male transsexuals were seeking a freedom only possible in patriarchy, and so was I. The means were different, but the impulses were related. I haven't changed my mind.[5]

Yet there is the most infamous TERF text of the twentieth century, and there is Andrea Dworkin's name on the cover. *Woman Hating* was published in 1974; *The Transsexual Empire* was published in 1979. Somehow, over the space of just five years, feminism's second wave shifted from a movement that was relatively accepting of trans people to a movement that was based on their exclusion and even their elimination from public life.

The Transsexual Empire comes out of a history of deep and scarring conflict over the inclusion of trans women in radical feminist spaces. Two women, specifically, became lightning rods: Sandy Stone, who worked as a sound engineer at the "women's music" label Olivia Records, was subject to bomb threats and death threats until she eventually quit her job. Beth Elliott, a trans lesbian folksinger who was scheduled to perform at the West Coast Lesbian Conference, became the center of an epic trashing, including an infamous speech at the podium from Robin Morgan.

"I will not call a male 'she'," Morgan said. "Thirty-two years of suffering in this androcentric society and of surviving, have earned me the title 'woman'; one walk down the street by a male transvestite, five minutes of his being hassled (which he may enjoy), and then he dares, he dares to think he understands our pain?"[6] Morgan called Elliott "an opportunist, an infiltrator, and a destroyer—with the mentality of a rapist," and ended her speech with what many people in the crowd heard as an unmistakable call for violence: "You know who he is. Now, you can let him into your workshops—or you can deal with him."[7]

This was the line: Trans women were men, and men were violent, and because trans women were violent (because men were violent), cis women were encouraged and permitted to be violent toward trans women.

To be clear: Hating trans women is not "man-hating." It's woman-hating, and specifically transmisogyny. Trans women aren't men; they're women. Even if you define "woman" in the most reductive way, as the set of people who experience a certain type of discrimination, trans women fit that definition. One defining factor of "women's oppression," for example, is increased vulnerability to sexual assault; trans women experience sexual violence at a higher rate than cis women. Another factor is the gender pay gap, intended to keep women sexually available to men by making them economically dependent on sex work or heterosexual marriage: There is a pay gap between trans women and cis men, between trans women and cis women, even between trans women and trans men, with trans women being at the bottom of every equation.

None of this, however, has stopped certain feminists from leveraging essentialist stereotypes of men against trans women. The patriarchal binary's masculine stereotypes—strong, assertive, dominating, sexually potent, etc.—are really meant to be traits of leadership, and as such, they're only deemed appropriate in cis, straight white men. When you take all those traits away from society's designated rulers, and project them onto the body of the Other, what you get looks like a monster: Hulking, violent, domineering, power hungry, sexually predatory.

Trans women aren't the only women to get hit with these stereotypes. Violence aimed against Black men by white people often rests on hyper-masculinizing them: Big, scary, aggressive, criminal. Yet negative stereotypes of Black women also subtly or not-so-subtly masculinize them: Pushy, angry, bossy, hypersexual. In much the same way, the violence aimed at trans women rests on stripping away their femininity and casting them as out-of-control male predators. It's a rhetorical strategy used by those in power to cast marginalized people as threatening, and to justify the violence done to them. Once you have cast another human being in the role of Dragon, you can cast yourself as the Hero who slays them and saves the village. This is what the trans-exclusive feminists of the second wave set out to do.

RED FLAGS, YARDSTICKS, AND LINES

Dworkin is not the only famous feminist associated with *The Transsexual Empire*. Supportive conversations with Adrienne Rich are cited throughout the work. I managed to read and cite Robin Morgan for years without learning her history with Beth Elliott. It is impossible to completely jettison these women from the canon—I defy you to spend a single day on the queer internet without encountering Adrienne Rich's concept of "compulsory heterosexuality," for example—but it's also impossible to excuse their transphobia.

"It's important to know when certain ideas are born from the same poisoned fruit that has given birth to other hideous ideas," says Gillian Branstetter—but that doesn't always necessitate ditching the whole theoretical framework.

Branstetter is a trans feminist advocate with a dazzlingly encyclopedic knowledge of feminist history. Her work has been a guidepost for me, because she's able to highlight the most useful parts of second-wave theory without excusing its uglier undercurrents. How, I asked her, do you draw the line between highlighting the useful aspects of a problematic work and whitewashing them? How do you distinguish an argument that is merely flawed from one that inevitably leads toward bigotry?

"Part of it is identifying the principles that are paving those bad roads," Branstetter says. "So, essentialist understandings of identity, rejection of other people's self-determination."

Framing feminism as a battle of All Women against All Men often leads to predictably bad places: "Sarah Huckabee Sanders, is she acting on hatred of women? No, she's acting in enforcement of a patriarchal understanding of the world," Branstetter says. Someone who isn't thinking in terms of that overarching patriarchal structure is more likely to land on a trans-antagonistic position.

A similar yardstick was put forth by Joanna Wuest, in the anthology *Feminism Against Cisness*. Feminisms that focused exclusively on "protecting" women from male aggression, Wuest wrote, dovetailed with conservative ideas of women as "the weaker sex"; adopting the language and strategy of those movements helped conservatives sell their anti-trans agenda "under the banner of protecting women and locking up male predators."[*]

Lest you think this is newfangled trans-rights-activist talk, Margaret Atwood talks about this in *The Handmaid's Tale* as the distinction between "freedom from" and "freedom to." She, too, argued that the politics of freedom-from lead toward Gilead, and only freedom-to gets you truly free.

---

[*] *Feminism Against Cisness*, ed. Emma Heaney, p. 176.

Transmisogyny was absolutely not second-wave consensus. The Olivia Records collective stood behind Sandy Stone, and raised the funds for her medical transition.[8] At the West Coast Lesbian Conference, a majority of the audience stood behind Beth Elliott; a popular vote resolved 3 to 1 in favor of letting her perform.[9] Cell 16—the first feminist separatist group, which advised women to renounce sex with men and focus on learning karate, and whose members terrified even other radfems with their militancy—included trans women; when they were targeted by anti-trans feminists for doing so, they shut down rather than kick their trans sisters out.[10]

None of this changed the outcome for Sandy Stone or Beth Elliott, both of whom eventually left the lesbian feminist community for their own safety. But the linkage of second-wave and radical feminism with transphobia was really not inevitable. It could have gone either way.

Janice Raymond pointed it in the wrong direction. Where Dworkin wrote that the goal of feminism was to eliminate transphobia, *The Transsexual Empire* explicitly says that the goal is to eliminate trans people: "I contend that the problem of transsexualism would best be served by morally mandating it out of existence." Sandy Stone, in particular, is the unnamed subject of nearly every page of *Empire*. In Chapter 4—which is devoted to the "problem" of trans women in lesbian feminist spaces; it's the one Dworkin is specifically credited with consulting on—Raymond just plain names her: "I feel raped when Olivia passes off Sandy [Stone], a transsexual, as a real woman. After all his male privilege, is he going to cash in on lesbian feminist culture too?" she quotes an anonymous sister as saying. "All transsexuals rape women's bodies by reducing the real female form to an artifact, appropriating this body for themselves," Raymond concurs. "However, the transsexually constructed lesbian-feminist violates women's sexuality and spirit, as well." .

So, trans women were "raping" feminism simply by interacting with other feminists. The only way to disprove claims about their "aggressive," "invasive" male nature was to leave, in total silence and without protesting—to push back against the abuse was proof that they deserved the abuse, and thus, further grounds for being forced out. "One would think that if [Sandy] Stone's commitment to and identification with women were genuinely woman-centered, he would have removed himself from Olivia and assumed some responsibility for the divisiveness,"[11] wrote Raymond. Or: "If I was really a woman, I'd be too sensitive and aware to claim to be a woman," as Beth Elliott wrote in her memoir, *Mirrors*.

Elliott read *The Transsexual Empire* from her exile; she called it "the *Mein Kampf* of anti-transsexual feminists."

"To call it sleazy hate literature would be too kind," she wrote in *Mirrors*. "It literally made me puke . . . What it did for me was to strip me of my last vestiges of belief that women, as women, were somehow better than the racists, anti-Semites, homophobes and woman-haters we oppose with such a valor."

Worse, Elliott wrote, "it's been used to intimidate the community into using opposition to transsexuals as a feminist litmus test." As Elliott well knew, trans women's greatest vulnerability in feminist circles was not bigots, but tepid allies who just wanted the fighting to stop: "If someone like this is going to be divisive because of what some women feel, they don't belong," she remembers hearing. "I mean, I guess I don't feel strongly about transsexuals either way, but why spoil women's space?"[12]

"Women's space" had already been ruined for women like Sandy Stone and Beth Elliott. But then, they didn't count as "women" anymore—that was the point.

So the trans possibilities of the second wave were foreclosed and forgotten—including, sometimes, by the women who had been their loudest proponents. In her final book, *Heartbreak*, Andrea Dworkin was writing about trans people again—trans men, this time. As far as I know, it's her only public statement on us. It starts off with her fulminating against the sex radicals: "There were so-called feminists who published in *Playboy*, *Hustler*, and *Penthouse* and penned direct attacks on feminists fighting pornography and prostitution." Indeed, there were, but that's not the important part. Here it is: "One at least has become a male through surgery—her head and heart were always right there."[13]

To be a trans man is to be a "her" gone wrong; to be a trans man is to be an anti-feminist pervert; a "male" heart is a bad heart and it's my fault for having one. Now, maybe, we can talk about how anti-trans feminists treat the lost "sisters" they so want trans guys to be.

2

TRANS MEN

"I WAS A TRUE BELIEVER," SAYS KY SCHEVERS, OF HER years as a conversion therapy advocate. "I really thought I was helping people."

Transphobic radical feminism is still around in the present day. The project of morally mandating trans people out of existence is still ongoing, and it targets trans people of all genders. The same logic that casts trans women as violent "male" intruders in feminist community also casts transmasculine people as lost and brainwashed "women" who must be brought back into the feminist fold at all costs. That process, though it's undertaken in the name of sisterhood, can be exceptionally violent, as Schevers soon found out.

Schevers is a transmasculine butch, she/her pronouns. It's a complicated identity, and it took her some time to figure it out—first, some time spent living as a trans man, then a growing sense of herself as genderqueer, then a realization that "dyke" was an important piece of herself that she needed to honor.

There are lots of people in the queer community who stop transitioning, or who redefine their identities over the course of their transitions, and there always have been. *Stone Butch Blues*, Leslie Feinberg's most famous work, is about a transmasculine butch who starts and then stops testosterone, sometimes living as a man, sometimes not.

It was on a trans-friendly message board for such people that Schevers was radicalized. "I made a post and a detransitioned woman who turned out to be very TERFy ended up replying," Schevers recalls. They began talking privately, and the idea of creating support groups specifically for what they called "detransitioned women" or "detransitioned radical feminism" came up.

The line adopted by these detransitioned women was familiar: Transmasculinity was a form of internalized misogyny. Transmasculine people felt they needed to transition because they were too traumatized (from rape, from sexual violence, from harassment) or too self-loathing (from beauty standards, from gender stereotypes, from life in patriarchy) to bear life as women.

"Because we believed that dysphoria was caused by trauma and living in a patriarchy, we also believed that it could be a chronic condition that one could learn to manage, like how people manage living with depression or PTSD," Schevers says. "Dysphoria was often compared to an addiction that could resurface or get worse under times of stress."

Radical feminism was the methadone that would keep transmasculine people from slipping back into their old habits and/or genders. If you learned enough feminist theory, and worked to expand the definition of womanhood from the inside, your gender dysphoria would magically become livable. If it didn't, you weren't yet feminist enough to feel it working.

The program was a hit. Radical feminist groups for "detransitioned women" began to crop up, online and off. Schevers led workshops at MichFest—the notoriously trans-exclusionary women's music festival—on the evils of trans ideology. She gave quotes to anti-trans journalists for articles that (she knew, even at the time) were intended to present transmasculinity as a harmful fad seducing the nation's girls. She lied to the reporters to make sure they'd get the quotes they needed.

"We thought we had special insight. We thought we were better than trans people," Schevers says. "Like, you know, we had figured things out, but they're still delusional."

Converting self-doubting trans guys into anti-trans activists is, objectively, a horrible thing to do. Yet it's worth pausing, for a moment, to consider why these programs were so effective.

There have always been ties between transmasculine people and lesbian feminism: "Some of those women turning trannie boy have been hardcore separatists," Beth Elliott wrote in 1996. Much of the distrust between trans men and trans women comes out of this history: Trans men were often still welcomed in the same "women's spaces" that were keeping trans women out. Calling MichFest "trans-exclusive," for example, is something of a misnomer; for years, it admitted trans men, even as it excluded trans women from its premises.

OUTSIDE THE GATES

Any discussion of MichFest must also be a discussion of Camp Trans, the alternate festival set up outside the MichFest's gates to protest its transphobia after a trans woman named Nancy Burkholder was twice kicked out of the main festival.

The first time Burkholder was ejected, in 1991, it was in the middle of the night, and she was left to find her way back to town on foot. The second time, in 1993, it was because she had set up a booth on the festival grounds to educate pass-ersby on trans issues; after she was kicked out, she set up her booth again, right outside the festival, and that was where Camp Trans set up shop in the following years.

The first Camp Trans was organized by Riki Anne Wilchins and Leslie Feinberg in 1994. After a five-year hiatus, the camp came back in 1999, organized by Feinberg, Wilchins and the Transsexual Menace, and the Boston and Chicago chapters of the Lesbian Avengers. The latter group included then-twenty-year-old Simon Fisher, who served as the lead organizer of Camp Trans until 2005.

By the late 1990s, the sex wars between anti-porn and sex-radical feminists had pretty much ended, and the sex-radical side had won. Queer punk was thriving, and literature of the day, like the 1997 anthology *Pomosexuals*, touted queerness's endless potential to break down and fuck with the gender binary. Thus, as Fisher recalls, pretty much anyone who protested at Camp Trans was organized under the banner of "dyke."

"The umbrella of the word 'dyke' was very broad," Fisher tells me. "Trans guys and trans women were both dykes. Like, this was fine. Trans fags were dykes. It was like, everyone's fine. Everyone's great. We're all just great. And this was a very gender utopian moment that quickly ended, but at the time that seemed very possible."

Which is all to say: If much TERFism came from within the lesbian feminist community, so did nearly all of the resistance. Even before Camp Trans, there were second-wave lesbian feminists—like the women of Olivia Records, who stood behind Sandy Stone, or Jeanne Cordova of the *Lesbian Tide*—who fought for and with trans women until the bitter end.

Words like "lesbian" and "feminist" and "queer" and "trans" shift and slide around in history; they mean different things at different times; they align and re-align along different axes. But within queer culture, there is both bigotry and resistance, whereas outside, in the dominant culture, trans people and cis queers are both regarded as a threat to stomp out.

———

IN TURN, RADICAL feminism has always had a certain respect for what I will begrudgingly call "female masculinity." Schevers herself says that she was drawn to the movement because it was one of the only places she could meet people who had similar gender presentations to her own: "They were very butch. They were very gender non-conforming. Some of them, probably, if they weren't so transphobic, maybe they would have identified as genderqueer or transmasculine."

Schevers is far from the first person to make this connection. One of the weirder elements of contemporary "gender-critical" rhetoric is just how often transphobic women will compare themselves to, identify with, or just plain say they *are* transmasculine people who never got around to transitioning.

"I've wondered whether, if I'd been born 30 years later, I too might have tried to transition,"[14] writes J. K. Rowling, who (let's just note, for the sake of complete accuracy) went by her initials in her first publications to avoid being read as female, and whose Twitter bio currently specifies that she is "sometimes known as Robert."[15] You can find the same sentiment all over the gender-critical internet: "I sometimes think I would have been labelled trans as a kid. I HATED girly stuff. Only wanted to wear trousers. Didn't like dolls, pink etc. Had short hair. I even used to say I wanted to be a boy," writes one Mumsnet user. "I spent 2 years at peak puberty time, wondering if I was a boy, and it Horrifies me that had it been now I would have been transed. My parents told me that of course I couldn't be a boy and then left me to figure it out," writes another user, who estimates that "I bet more than half the women on this board came to a peak moment thinking exactly this."[16]

We will never actually know whether all these trans-exclusive feminists are closeted transmasculine people. (Although, if they are, a whole lot of "feminist" transphobia comes down to trans men being violently misogynistic to trans women.) What we can say, though, is that trans-exclusive feminists tend to see transmasculine people as failed versions of themselves—they believe we are trying to escape patriarchy, just like feminists, but doing it the wrong way, becoming the oppressor rather than fighting the oppression.

"Saving" transmasculine people thus comes down to convincing them that they are betraying the feminist cause by existing: "The idea that if you retransitioned you'd be hurting other women and giving into patriarchy was used to control people and keep them in line," Schevers tells me. It turns out that it is very, very easy to make trans men feel guilty about being men.

Transmasculine guilt is a raw subject. Nearly every trans man I've interviewed has brought it up. Trans men know full well how this world treats women, and now, we have to come forward and tell the women in our lives that we share a gender with their oppressors and abusers. No matter how necessary it is, it's scary, and it feels like betraying them. Many trans men have delayed their transitions for years or even decades out of fear of becoming "the enemy"; others wonder if they're evil for "wanting to be men," when men are so clearly terrible. You can find this reflected in the literature for as long as there has *been* transmasculine literature: "Many FTMs wonder if all men are jerks and are disturbed by hegemonic masculinity. This becomes a significant barrier to achieving an untroubled identification as a man,"[17] Henry Rubin wrote in *Self-Made Men*, one of the first books ever published on the subject, way back in 2003.

Transition can also cut us off from support networks we took for granted pre-transition. When transmasculine people begin to look like cis men (if we ever do—and not all of us do), people start to assume we've never experienced gendered oppression. "Society has always avoided thinking about trans men because it can easily be justified as 'treating them like any other man,'" writes Oliver Reeson, in a 2019 essay for *The Lifted Brow*. There is "a flattening out of your history, the expectation that you should forget a life-long relationship with oppression because, provisionally, it doesn't appear to apply."[18] The harm and trauma we experienced is still part of us, and it still hurts, and we may even still be vulnerable to sexism or misogyny in some contexts, but in the wider world, those experiences are dismissed.

How all this is intended, I cannot say. What it feels like, though, is all your friends suddenly giving up on you, or seeing you as a traitor and an enemy, based on something you couldn't control and didn't choose. The "detransitioned women" took a population struggling with isolation, rejection, guilt, and shame, and offered them community, solidarity, a sense of belonging, and even a pathway to redemption, in the form of converting other trans mascs and spreading the radical feminist gospel. It was massively harmful, but this is also just how cults work.

One thing they did not do, however, was cure anyone's dysphoria. Even as she was busy saving souls for the matriarchy, Schevers could not help seeing that many of the transmasculine people she worked with were still dysphoric—they weren't becoming any less trans, as the result of being more feminist, and those feelings were becoming steadily more painful as they were repressed. Her own dysphoria, in particular, wasn't going anywhere, no matter how much work she did or how fervently she believed in it.

"You can only suffer for so long until you ask yourself if it's really worth it and if your suffering is really making the world a better place," Schevers said. She found herself reading books by "ex-gays" who had attempted to make themselves heterosexual by embracing evangelical Christianity. Line by line, tactic by tactic, those stories tracked with the conversion therapy she'd been calling "feminism"; for trans men, no differently than for cis gay men, it would never work.

It's obvious that Schevers deeply regrets her involvement with this movement. She's spent the past several years as a hate researcher, using her familiarity with TERF movements to explain their tactics and organizing to the outside world. Yet she also says, over and over, that she was looking for a way to express and receive "compassion."

So here's my question: How different would this story look if actual compassion had been available—for Schevers, and for all the other transmasculine people like her? Transmasculine people do need support networks; they do need solidarity; they do need a feminist way to do masculinity or manhood, and they need all this badly enough that some of them will hurt themselves and others trying to get it.

Where do we find the theory that teaches us how to be trans, *and* men, *and* feminists, all at the same time, without rejecting or denying any part of ourselves? As it turns out, feminists have been trying to create it all along.

3

JOHN STOLTENBERG

"I THINK IT WAS ON TWITTER THAT I REFERRED TO CHELsea Manning as 'she,'" John Stoltenberg tells me. "And someone got back to me and said, you know, 'she!?' Exclamation mark. Question mark. And I engaged with this person, not knowing what I was getting into, and it turns out I was walking into an onslaught of vitriol."

Stoltenberg is radical feminism's resident masculinity expert. He's been writing about the social construction of manhood within patriarchy for decades. His most famous book, 1989's *Refusing to Be a Man*, argues that "without systemic male dominance, no-one can believably be a man"; the political hierarchy of gender constructs "man" solely as the person who is on top, in control, entitled to and violent toward the bodies of women, and thus, anyone who fails to get with the program is less than a man in the eyes of society.

For Stoltenberg, this is a good thing. He foresees a whole coalition of marginalized men—queer men; men who are survivors of sexual violence; men with close ties to feminist communities—claiming an identity on the margins of patriarchal "manhood";

some "moral identity that could be claimed and embodied unabashedly by people born with a penis."

Those last four words are, let's say, outdated. They're also not very representative of Stoltenberg's thinking: He's adamant throughout his work that gender and sex are not binary. Humans "don't just come in XX or XY; they also come in XXY and XYY and XXX," with "a vast range of genital formations." In his utopia, humans "*have* sex. They do not have *a* sex." Belief in biological supremacy lays the grounds for a definition of "manhood" that is all about force and punching down: "Male supremacy is not rooted in any natural order," he tells us. "Rather, it has been socially constructed, socially created, *especially through a socially constructed belief in what a sex is, how many there are, and who belongs to which.*"[19] [my emphasis]

In an age when everyone and their dog has an opinion on "positive masculinity" and how to rescue our boys from the manosphere, it's startling to realize that someone has been doing this work within feminism—and even within radical feminism—for decades. Yet you almost certainly don't know John Stoltenberg as the author of *Refusing to be a Man*. You know him, if you know him at all, as Andrea Dworkin's husband—the man who lived and worked with her for thirty years. In this, too, he has proven to be ahead of his time.

A few years ago, Stoltenberg began to publish essays, like 2021's "Andrea Dworkin Was Not Transphobic," in which he—politely, reasonably—maintains that Dworkin, who did not believe in binary sex, would not have organized around "women's sex-based rights" or "biological" womanhood. "I am certain she would not ally herself with any view that furthers 'biological superiority,' which she considered 'the world's most dangerous and deadly idea,'"[20] he wrote. As evidence of how seriously he takes this mission, I should tell you that he sometimes goes door to door: Some years ago, when I offhandedly referred to Dworkin as a TERF in an article, I received an email from Stoltenberg setting me straight.

This approach did not endear him to his radical feminist peers. "Shit came out of the sewers," Stoltenberg told me, on a Zoom call—one to which he graciously agreed, after I dug up that old email and asked him to expand on his thoughts. I can tell you now that his eyes are very blue, and that his voice is very gentle, and I can also tell you that he asked to retain an independent recording of this conversation, presumably as a safeguard against misrepresentation; he seems to me like someone who has been playing defense for a very long time.

That defense has been played against women he knew and worked with for most of his career. Julie Bindel, who is named in the acknowledgments for *Heartbreak*, now names Stoltenberg as the chief culprit in "the unforgivable transing of Andrea Dworkin."[21] Phyllis Chesler sniffs that "perhaps John is trans-channeling Andrea."[22] Janice Raymond wrote that "Stoltenberg joins the crowd of mansplainers who tell women that we don't know what we are doing."[23]

Stoltenberg himself has a hard time accepting that their hatred is not just a misunderstanding. "It took me a while to learn how to live in this world with all these haters coming at me, because I would try to sincerely engage. I would try to explain myself,"

Stoltenberg says. "I still would like to. I still believe that there's an explanation that could unhinge this . . . this *mania*."

It's hard for me to believe this, just as it's hard for me to believe Stoltenberg's justification for the Raymond blurb. (He said that Dworkin intended to protest nonconsensual medical experimentation; I told him that he could read *Histories of the Transgender Child* for a better and more responsible history.) I engaged with Stoltenberg fully expecting that he might be running apologetics for his beloved partner.

Yet Stoltenberg has been actively trying to do the work of trans inclusion for a long time. He's engaged in public dialogues with trans feminists. He has published calls for trans and cis feminist movements to work in solidarity: "Everyone who takes a gender off-ramp wants to go someplace else where they can safely be themself," he writes. "Let's listen carefully and respectfully and see whether our stories—which are, after all, about the same white- and male-supremacist superhighway—have more in common than we know."[24] He has continued to do this, for very little reward, and at great personal risk, because he thinks it matters.

I genuinely did try to pick the guy apart, to find the transphobic loophole hidden somewhere inside his philosophy—again, the idea that "man" *only* represents a dominant position within patriarchy doesn't leave a lot of room for trans men to exist as "real" men, and it implicitly casts us as deluded would-be oppressors. It also fails to account for the real and urgent pain of gender dysphoria. In his post-patriarchal utopia, I asked Stoltenberg, would there still be people who identify as men and women? Would medical transition still happen, or is he arguing, as the anti-trans conversion therapists do, that removing gender oppression would make gender dysphoria cease to exist?

"I think it's perfectly serviceable for the human species to have a sorting system," Stoltenberg says. "But not a ranking system based on it." He is opposed to gender as a power structure, in other words, rather than gender as identity. As for medical transition, he doesn't see a future where it never happens: "The interiority of one's bodily experience does have a relationship to sense of self and presentation. That, I think, is apart from what I'm referring to as the dominant ethic that requires putting somebody down in order to be [a 'real' man]."

The poet and novelist Roz Kaveney is a trans woman who spent the 1980s doing battle with Dworkin over her stances on pornography and sex work: In her review of Dworkin's semi-autobiographical novel, *Mercy*, she called the protagonist a "self-regarding and self-constructed figure that calls women together in a crusade of pointless retributive violence," and argued that Dworkin's lack of feminist solidarity was manifest in "the contemptuous way she endeavours to manipulate her women readers with rhetorical trickery."[25] Yet when I asked, Kaveney told me that "[Dworkin's] endorsement of Raymond seems to have been a glitch," and credited Stoltenberg, specifically, with Dworkin's relatively enlightened stance: "Stoltenberg is key," she told me. "He was her lifeline, I think."

So I will not swear that every single reader of this book would agree with Stoltenberg's politics—if your beef with Dworkin is about pornography, for example, he agrees with her—but I believe he genuinely wants a feminist future with trans people in it. That shouldn't be a high bar to clear. As of this writing, it still is.

TERFS AND SWERFS

Dworkin's stance on sex work does not get much space here, but it is not a minor issue for the trans community. Her most well-known effort, the 1983 Dworkin-MacKinnon Anti-Pornography Civil Rights Ordinance, was not explicitly intended to be transphobic—Stoltenberg notes that trans people, like women, were named as a protected class therein—but its framework was immediately, and eagerly, adopted by the Reagan administration in its own quest to ban transgressive sexual content.

Basically: Queer people are disproportionately likely to be affected by censorship of "offensive" sexual content, because the dominant culture finds our sexualities offensive. Trans people—as you may have learned from Florence Ashley's story of their selfies being non-consensually uploaded onto porn sites—are so hypersexualized that our very existence is often seen as pornographic. We carry this legacy today in, say, the right-wing quest to ban Maia Kobabe's graphic novel *Gender Queer* on the grounds of its "pornographic" content (which consists of a single non-explicit drawing of a blow job) or the Heritage

Foundation's classification of "trans ideology" as *de facto* pornography.

There is also the fact that trans people, particularly trans women, are overwhelmingly more likely to be involved in sex work than cis women, because it is one of the few lines of work open to them. Sylvia Rivera—who, in her own estimation, threw not the first but the second brick at Stonewall—spoke in 2001 about trans women being shamed at Pride ceremonies for wearing makeup and miniskirts.

"Excuse me! It goes with the business that we're in at that time!" Rivera said. "We don't want to be out there sucking dick and getting fucked in the ass. But that's the only alternative we have to survive because the laws do not give us the right to go and get a job the way we feel comfortable. I do not want to go to work looking like a man when I know I am not a man."[*]

Sex-worker exclusionary feminists, also known as SWERFs, often claimed to want to "save" women like Sylvia, but in fact, they rarely even listened to them, and have pursued criminalization measures that overwhelmingly render sex workers vulnerable to abuse, assault, and rape,

---

[*] *We Want It All: An Anthology of Radical Trans Poetics*, pp. 385–386.

often at the hands of the police enforcing these supposedly "feminist" laws. Most sex worker advocates today endorse full decriminalization of consensual sex work. So does Amnesty International: There is empirical evidence that decriminalization has reduced violence against sex workers everywhere it has been tried.[†]

This approach does not conflict with the belief that porn or the sex industry are misogynistic. It's a question of which measures are most effective in reducing violence and exploitation: "As feminists, we know the misogyny and violence we've experienced in the sex trade to be abhorrent," write Juno Mac and Molly Smith, in their 2018 book *Revolting Prostitutes*. "But the humane abolition of sex work can only happen when marginalized people no longer have to sustain themselves through the sex industry; when it is no longer necessary for their survival."[‡]

This is a long and heated debate, and I have hardly scratched its surface. Just know that, at one point, it took up much more space in this

---

[†] "Amnesty International Publishes Policy and Research on Sex Workers' Rights," Amnesty International, May 26, 2016.

[‡] *Revolting Prostitutes: The Fight for Sex Workers' Rights*, Juno Mac and Molly Smith, p. 208.

chapter, and that *Revolting Prostitutes* is an excellent resource for anyone who wants to explore it in depth.

TALKING TO STOLTENBERG, I found myself thinking about how little any pre-conceived narrative about "men" could have prepared me for the human being on the other end of this conversation. Though I believe Stoltenberg has a much more complex and conscious relationship with gender than the average man, or the average cis person ("I'm really into this whole anti-binary movement," he tells me at one point) a tremendous amount of the feminist dismissal aimed at him hinges on the idea that he is just somebody's boyfriend, not a voice worth listening to in his own right. Yet he is the second-wave figure who's been willing to do what so many of Beth Elliott's friends wouldn't: Stand up, burn bridges, make a ruckus about trans people's rightful place in feminism.

Before I end the Zoom call, I ask Stoltenberg if there's anything he wants to add. "I think I just want to pose a question to you," he says. "I would be very interested, through your lens, to see what you see about men."

He's the first person to ask me that. No: He's the *only* person to ask me that. I've been called to the carpet to defend my gender over and over. I've been subjected to dozens or hundreds of strangers' ideas of what a "man" is, and why I'm bad for being a man, or bad for not really being one. No one has ever looked past their own definition of manhood to ask how I, personally, define *man*, or why it's important to call myself one.

There are a million answers I could give him. Maybe I'm interested in stealing the label of "man" out from under the men who use it as a license to kill. Maybe I just think it's hot when boys kiss. Maybe I want to experience everything that it's possible to experience in one human form, and exploring many different gender expressions is part of that. Maybe I looked down at myself in second-grade gym class and realized I was supposed to be born a boy, then waited thirty years until I figured out how to correct the error. Maybe I use the word "man" because there are no better words for what I am yet. Maybe I use the word "man" to change what that word means.

Maybe some of these things, or all of them, or none of them are true. You will never know, until you ask me—none of us will ever know how anyone else experiences gender, until we are willing to ask the question, and willing to listen to the answers we get. Traditional narratives about where men fit into the feminist movement do very little to account for John Stoltenberg. Though I may disagree with him on some points, I respect that—because traditional narratives about where men fit into the feminist movement do pretty much nothing to account for me.

4

ON NOT REFUSING
TO BE A MAN

THERE WAS A TIME, AT THE VERY BEGINNING OF MY TRANsition, when I thought that being a feminist and a man was easy. Being a man (I believed) gave you Male Privilege, and in order to be a feminist, you had to Own Your Male Privilege, and then work against it. Just that one thing—owning privilege, disavowing privilege—was all any man had to do to be a decent feminist, or a decent person. I said this over, and over, and I said it in tones of tremendous confidence, and I could not for the life of me understand why every trans guy who'd been out for longer than about six seconds rolled his eyes at me, or sighed, or walked away.

The truth—I now know—is that "male privilege" can be a nebulous thing for trans guys. In order to work against it, you first need to know that you have it, and it's not always certain that you do.

Here's what I mean: I once took an early train to New York. It left before dawn, and I started nodding off on board. At first, I tried to stop myself—the first time I fell asleep on public transit was on a Greyhound bus, when I was sixteen years old, and I woke up to find my male seatmate's hand in my crotch—but then I realized that, looking the way I look now, there was probably no reason to be worried. I wasn't a sixteen-year-old girl who had lost consciousness in public, I was just another middle-aged guy on a commuter train, and as such, I could close my eyes. So I did, guiltily enjoying the male privilege of letting my guard down.

But what if somebody clocked me? I thought, and my eyes popped right back open.

I was safe as long as people read me as a cis man, but if anyone figured out I was trans, I would be in more danger than ever—and much of that danger would stem from misogyny, the perception of me as a woman who had failed to comply to my "natural" role.

I would love to tell you that "male privilege" is obvious, and that you always know when you have it, and only bad people ever take advantage of it, because that would mean that I, a Good Person™, am always in the clear. But it's just not true. I have male privilege at some times, and I lack male privilege at other times, and unless I know exactly how everyone in a situation reads me, I can never really be sure whether I have it or not. Some days, I will just glide through life, noting that everyone has been strangely polite and no one has condescended to me or sexualized me or taken out their rage on me lately, and I'll feel like I must be doing something right. Then I'll realize what is happening, and I'll be appalled.

None of this means that I am innocent of misogyny. *Misogyny* is different from privilege. It's something anyone can do, from any social position, women very much included. As Thomas Page McBee writes of his own post-transition feminism, "the question wasn't if I was sexist, but how." *Everyone* in a patriarchy is sexist, at least sometimes, because all of us are taught to denigrate women and femininity. Sexism is not (just) the conscious decision to beat up or grope or insult a woman, it's "thousands of subtle behaviors performed unquestioningly by almost everyone of every gender."[26] You take responsibility where you find it. You stay on the lookout for your own bullshit. You clean it up.

So, no: Being a trans guy doesn't automatically prevent you from being sexist, or misogynistic, or abusive, or violent, or benefiting from the oppression of women. It's hard to argue that a transmasculine person has more Privilege than a cis woman—we have less of it, in most cases—but we are unambiguously privileged over trans women, and plenty of transmasculine people are complicit or active in transmisogyny. Trans men are men, and more than that, trans men are human. It is within every human being's power to suck.

But if trans guys believe it is impossible to live as a man while also living by their values, many of them will choose their values over their lives, and tremendous suffering will result. Hating ourselves for being men is the same as hating ourselves for being trans, and hating ourselves for being trans will kill us. Fundamentally, I don't believe most transmasculine people do transition into a life of unchecked masculine privilege. I believe they come to transition from histories of abuse, of sexual assault, of partner violence, of shame and denial and self-abnegation and self-hatred, and emerge into a new and even scarier form of oppression. Before those guys can successfully reckon with the power accorded to them as men or masculine people, they need to heal from the harm that has been done to them. Corny as it sounds, that healing requires self-compassion—trying to be a perfect "ally" to everyone else, without knowing how to take care of yourself, is just deferred self-harm.

So transmasculine people do need feminism; we need it to understand the harm done to us, as well as our own capacity to harm people. But that feminism needs to rest on something deeper than a belief that girls rule and boys drool. It needs to have some way to account for transmasculine people, other than casting us as self-loathing basket cases or power-hungry traitors to Womankind, or pretending that adding "he/him" pronouns to a social media bio magically renders someone invulnerable to all forms of gendered oppression.

If you are a woman, and you "hate men," or (as I suspect is

far more common) you find it important to openly voice your anger and criticism of men after a lifetime of being told to appease them at your own expense, I won't stop you. That anger is important. You're important. I have no right to judge you for it—not because I'm a man, but because I'm angry at men, too. I have spent large parts of my life furiously, incandescently angry at men and misogyny and patriarchy, and that anger was lifesaving: It inspired me to defend myself. It reminded me that I was a person worth defending.

Yet anger is not a plan. Anger is, at most, a sign that something needs fixing. Hatred is not a revolution—it is despair with a leather jacket and cool sunglasses. Gender essentialism—all men are like this, and all women are like that; all men are violent, and all women are victims; all men are dominant, and all women are dominated; all men are Bad, because they oppress women, and all women are Good, because they are oppressed by men—is not only wrong, it's incredibly fatalistic. When we buy into this worldview, we are buying into the idea that patriarchy is natural and inevitable, that men are eternally and inalterably monstrous, and thus, that nothing can ever change.

There is only one group of people that benefits from that belief, and it's not women. When we buy the line that men are inherently violent and oppressive, we miss the far grimmer truth: Men are violent and oppressive because they *choose* to be, because they want to be, because participating in the patriarchal binary rewards them and gives them power, and they don't want to give that up. All those horrible, hateful guys that I dealt with on the phone sex line—they weren't helpless slaves to their "male socialization," nor were they biologically programmed to be rude and cruel to service workers. They were full-grown human beings with agency who decided to hurt people. There's nothing inherently shameful about being a man, but it is *tremendously* shameful to be a bully, and that's the life they chose.

Men can choose differently. Men can be feminists, and some are—not nearly enough of them, not yet, but choosing the right thing is always just as possible as choosing the wrong one. The problem with seeing "men" as natural-born predators—great white sharks with khakis and favorite football teams—isn't that it fails to recognize the work of "good" men. They'll be fine, trust me. It's that it lets those bad men off the hook for the harm they do.

Every day that we wake up and fight patriarchy, we create new ways of doing gender—for everyone. Women will not be the only people to benefit, nor are they the only people responsible for making change. Anger at the status quo is normal; it is even necessary. But in the world we're building, no one will need to be angry at "men" any more. By the time we get there, everyone, including men, will be feminists, and feminism will be for everyone once again.

Part 5

LEAVING

I have lived long enough
to see my lost causes found.
—PAULI MURRAY

THE WEEK I SAT DOWN TO FINISH THIS BOOK, DONALD
Trump was elected president for the second time. It was not the
first time the book had been touched by disaster, but it was, by far,
the most destabilizing.

I wrote the book in a world that had trouble accepting trans
people. I did not yet believe that my country was committed to
eliminating them. I was worried about bad reviews, hate mail,
public humiliation; I was worried that my community would

think I was throwing them under the bus for cis feminist acceptance, or that cis feminists would respond to criticism with hostility and defensiveness. I was worried about offending people, or angering people, with the book I published. Then Trump won, and I was worried about whether it would still be legal to publish books by trans people at all.

The Trump campaign had spent its final weeks blanketing the country with anti-trans ads, some of them starkly obscene in their hatred—a picture of Dr. Rachel Levine, the trans woman who then served as Assistant Secretary to the Department of Health, dissolving into a picture of a clown smeared with red lipstick—making the suppression of trans people into Trump's central closing message. The campaign reportedly spent $215 million on anti-trans ads alone—as Gillian Branstetter noted, there are only 1.6 million trans adults in America, meaning that "the Trump campaign spent $134.38 on anti-trans ads for every single trans person that actually exists."[1]

They would not have gone all-in on this message unless they expected it to meet with popular support, and they got it: "About half of voters said support for transgender rights has gone too far,"[2] read one headline from the Associated Press. A quarter of those voters said the country's current level of support for trans rights was "about right"; only two in ten said that there was not enough support.

Every single trans person I know—every single trans person *alive*, give or take a Buck Angel—falls into that two in ten. We are so very, very vastly outnumbered.

It feels like a luxury to worry about *feminism* in this environment. It feels like nitpicking, to insist on naming different strands and varieties of feminism, and to sort out the strands most likely to cause harm. Fascism does not care whether someone is a liberal feminist or a socialist feminist or a queer sex-radical or a second-wave holdout or a transsexual communist or a transfeminist gender abolitionist or a pomosexual anarchist genderqueer. It cares that women and queers are talking without permission, and it puts them all down.

Frankly: With all the existential threats facing us right now, who has time to care about *feminism*? I mean: me, obviously. But who *else*? On the day the election was called for Trump, while doing a twenty-four-hour speed run of all my vices—a Nutella croissant from the bakery; buying pointless shit online; a cinnamon walnut babka from the bakery; posting too much on social media; a beer; posting too much on social media *after* the beer; finally, inevitably, arguing on social media—I found my answer. It was two sentences that the twenty-six-year-old white supremacist Nick Fuentes had posted on the site formerly known as Twitter, celebrating Trump's victory:

Your body, my choice. Forever.[3]

You know who cares about feminism? *That guy*. He cares about it tremendously. He has forged his politics and his public career around caring about it. He sees gender-marginalized people's control over their own bodies—your control over your body, my control over mine; gender transition, abortion, because they are and have always been the same issue—as a threat so profound that he is willing to plunge his own country into authoritarianism. Trump regained office precisely because many people feel the same way.

We need to care at least as much as they do. They will do anything it takes to destroy, immiserate and subjugate us—*forever*, like the man said—and we need to do everything in our power to make sure that doesn't happen.

That there is a "we," I have to believe. I need to think that heterosexual feminists and cisgender queers and trans people can stop jockeying for relative power within the patriarchal power structure and notice that patriarchy as a whole depends on keeping us down. Only 1.6 million adults in America are transgender, but 7.1 percent of us identify as LGBT,[4] and 50.5 percent of us are women,[5] and nearly *all* of us are oppressed and disadvantaged by the patriarchal gender binary.

If we could actually see each other as part of one cohesive constituency, we would have what it takes to change the world. We can move together or break apart, but those are the only two options. Right now, I don't know about you, but my world looks extremely broken.

In his book *Some Styles of Masculinity*, the artist and AIDS activist Gregg Bordowitz talks about "stigma," a concept he took from the 1963 book entitled (unsurprisingly) *Stigma*, by Erving Goffman. Bordowitz, channeling Goffman, says that there is "stigma that all kinds of people face, because of sexuality, race, ethnicity, ability, drug addiction, incarceration—they add up and add up." The only consistent thing about stigma is the fact that nearly everybody carries it: "The only unimpeachable identity in the United States in 1963 is a white male who's married to a woman, has children, and is good at sports. The only one!"

Our unimpeachable identities have not gotten any more varied over the years. But the sheer universality of stigma is its own kind of power: "How do you resist fascism? An army of the sick," Bordowitz tells us. "I believe that, if we take all the stigmas in the room, and if we all identify at the level of those stigmas, then we have a chance."[6]

There is a point where all our stigmas connect, where the lines between different identities (queer, trans, woman, poor, person of color, immigrant, incarcerated, disabled) dissolve and we all become simply Other. No matter what we are, the world sees us in terms of what we are not: We are *not* cis, straight white men with money. We are *not* the people who were intended to rule the world.

Yet that place, where marginalizations collide and blur, where forms of Otherness collect without being clearly labeled or separated, has given birth to some of the keenest insights into how oppression works. Before I leave you, I want to tell you about Pauli Murray.

———

IT IS HARD to imagine a feminist more stodgy and second-wave-liberal than Murray seems at first glance: A cofounder of the National Organization of Women (and, according to some sources, the person who came up with the idea in the first place), a personal friend of Eleanor Roosevelt, a legal scholar who is the credited source for Ruth Bader Ginsburg's arguments establishing sex-based discrimination as unconstitutional. Murray was also a civil rights activist of some renown, who took part in some of the earliest bus boycotts, and, as a law student, wrote the argument Thurgood Marshall used to overturn the "separate but equal" doctrine of *Plessy v. Ferguson*. Finally, Murray was a poet, whose work was read at Martin Luther King Jr.'s funeral.

Pauli Murray was trans. It's typically risky to assign a definite label like this to a deceased figure, but Pauli Murray is as clear-cut a case of a closeted transmasculine person as you are likely to find in the early twentieth century. They refused to wear feminine clothing from an early age. They occasionally lived as a young man or teenage boy—sometimes intentionally, when riding the rails cross-country, and sometimes even accidentally, as when an officer who arrested Murray during a protest marked them down as a boy named "Oliver." They sometimes published under male pseudonyms, and abridged their given name, Pauline, to the androgynous Pauli. Murray loved women, but did not identify as gay, saying that their feelings for their female partners were simply a heterosexual man's feelings for the women he loved. Throughout their young life, until middle age, Murray pleaded with doctors to put them on testosterone. When Harvard Law School rejected Murray's application because the school did not admit women, Murray responded by offering to transition: "Gentlemen, I would gladly change my sex to meet your requirements but since the way of such change has not been revealed to me, I have no recourse but to appeal to you to change your minds."[7]

Murray's transness was not the only way they slipped between societal categories, or even the most important one. Murray also came from a prominent Southern Black family, many of whose members were relatively light-skinned; several family members had left home to pass for white, including some of Murray's own siblings. Murray themself tended to slip between racial categories—in the South, Simon Fisher wrote, Murray was read as unambiguously Black, but in the North, people often weren't sure how to categorize them: They were taken for Indian, or Cuban, or any number of other not-exactly-white identities.

Murray moved through the world knowing that they could be perceived as either Black or non-Black, either male or female, either straight or gay, depending on the assumptions of the people around them. Murray wasn't intentionally fooling anyone—they were always just looking and acting like Pauli Murray—but that made no difference. People saw whatever they wanted or expected to see, and if Murray ever failed to anticipate their perceptions, brutal violence could result: "Oh God! My face has slipped them. / Can I endure the killing weight of time it takes them / To be sure?" Murray wrote, in a poem entitled "Mulatto's Dilemma."

"Racial and gender nonnormativity explicitly crossed paths on Murray's body, and as s/he walked through the world, others were always taking measure of this dual non belonging," Fisher writes. Eventually, this led Murray to believe that "both racialization and gendering are violent binary systems imposed from without . . . rather than truths that emerge from the body."[8]

Murray's legal work on gender and racial discrimination rested on their identification of race and gender as "arbitrary categories." Your perception of someone's race or gender could not give you any reliable information about who they were or what they were capable of, and thus, making a decision based on it was inherently discriminatory. It's an insight that has proved useful to many different marginalized communities, but it took Pauli Murray—who moved, every day, through other people's kaleidoscopic and frequently mistaken assumptions about their identity—to get there.

In time, this interest in blurry, shifting, and arbitrary categories became the foundation for Murray's great work: "Jane Crow," Murray's theory that Black women faced a specific form of oppression, not for being Black, nor for being women, but for being both at once. In the space where two identities fed into each other, some new identity arose and had to be dealt with on its own terms.

This insight, simple though it seems in retrospect, was foundational for all that followed: Murray's work on "Jane Crow" was a direct antecedent to Kimberle Crenshaw's theory of intersectionality. The Supreme Court's 2020 Bostock decision, which rendered it unconstitutional to discriminate against trans or queer people, was based directly on Murray's work. Feminist theory developed a way of thinking about complex identities because someone with a supremely complex identity was willing to share the insights they had gained by living between categories. People of color, women, trans people, queer people, are all still benefiting from Pauli Murray's work, even if we don't know this history, even if we've never heard Pauli Murray's name.

Putting a precise label on Murray's activism always feels confining: Were they a racial justice activist? (Yes.) An advocate for the working class? (Yes.) A feminist? (Yes.) A trans ancestor? (Yes.) Pauli Murray was, simply, Other, and they stood for the rights and dignity of the Other. Living between identities, they could reach out and touch them all.

As long as feminism has existed, trans people have been part of its story. The framework for treating trans and feminist identities as interconnected does not need to be invented—it has always been here, because we have always been here, creating it. The question is whether we will use it, or continue to widen a fissure between *trans* and *feminist* that never needed to exist in the first place.

So, before this book is over, I will add two more definitions of gender to the ever-mounting pile. Either one is a possible future. Which future you choose is up to you.

#4

GENDER AS TRAUMA

("BE A MAN.")

GENDER IS IMPOSED ON US FROM THE MOMENT WE CAN breathe. It controls and determines our relationships, our jobs, our families, our every waking moment. Gender tells us which toys we can play with, and who we can befriend, and what kind of sex we can have, and with whom, and under what conditions; gender tells you where you're allowed to go and what you're allowed to say and what your hair and hands and home and clothes and posture have to look like.

The price for breaking any single one of these rules is violence. Do gender wrong, and people will ostracize you; they will isolate you; they will shout slurs at you; they will dehumanize and demonize you. People—including your own parents—will beat you. People—including your own partners—will rape you. Some people will kill you or try to kill you. Other people, many more people—politicians, celebrities, feminists, etc.—will come up with reasons to have you killed.

Gender is a trauma. There is no way for it *not* to be a trauma in a patriarchy where it is coercively imposed from birth. Any person who expected to exercise the constant, meticulous, bodily control of other human beings that Gender does, or who punished defiance and mistakes with the same violence, would be a murderer, a rapist, the worst kind of abuser. That violence and control don't get any easier for the individual body and psyche to bear if they come from a faceless structural force.

Gender is traumatic for men as well as women, cis people as well as trans people, because all of us live under its control; none of us have the ability to opt out of it. No one's gender can be consensual unless everyone gets to choose.

The feminist movement, when viewed from a certain angle, looks like a vast archive of unacknowledged and untreated trauma. Shulamith Firestone spent her adult life floating in and out of mental institutions, and eventually starved to death in her own apartment. Valerie Solanas, Firestone's neighbor, never saw a dime from the *SCUM Manifesto* that made her famous; after shooting Andy Warhol, her mental health collapsed, her allies deserted her, and she wound up living on the streets, known to the local police as "Scab Lady" because she compulsively dug into her flesh with a fork. Andrea Dworkin spent her last years in a downward spiral of physical and mental health crises, taking upwards of twelve pills just to sleep at night, and died of heart failure at the age of fifty-two: "I'm simply used up," she wrote to Catherine McKinnon a few years before her death. "I feel virtually nothing except sometimes pain."[9]

This is what trauma does: Uses us up, wears us down, makes us sick. Post-traumatic stress is not a mental illness, but a physical injury; if the body experiences a threat that is terrifying or inescapable enough to overwhelm its defense mechanisms, it remains stuck in a state of permanent high alert. The rape, the car crash, the war, the beating, the chronically abusive home; they never end, not for our bodies. We live inside one intolerable moment forever, pushed into a state of primal terror every time we are reminded of the original incident.

The human body is not built to live on high alert every moment of every day. The stress wears you down, depletes your resources, results, not only in mental distress, but in heart disease, high blood pressure, chronic respiratory disease, early dementia, arthritis. Feminists—turned into a lightning rod for all this culture's hatred of women—often live like the cleanup workers at Chernobyl, exposing themselves to the worst of society's violence in the name of fixing it, cleaning up the poison that is seeping into their bones.

Trans people also live in a state of pervasive trauma, whether or not we choose to be activists. There is no other way to live under a gender regime dedicated to making sure we do not exist. Eighty percent of transgender adults living in America have experienced suicidal ideation, and 40 percent of us have actually attempted suicide.[10] Forty-two percent of transgender people meet the clinical criteria for post-traumatic stress disorder. In the general population, that figure is 4.7 percent.[11]

How cruel it is, then, that so much anti-trans activism sells itself by piously triggering women's trauma while pretending to heal it: Women need to be *protected* from trans women on sports teams. Women need to be *protected* from trans women in locker rooms. Women need to be *protected* from trans women in prisons, in bathrooms, on the street, anywhere, forever, and if anyone you think is a woman or a girl turns out to be transmasculine, and transitions, then they're clearly doing it because they weren't *protected* from male oppression, so you need to convert and detransition them to *protect* them from themselves.

Women need to be *protected*, *protected*, *protected*, and the threat at the end of the line is always rape, it is always battery, it is always male violence. The problem here is not only that trans people are just as vulnerable to male violence as cis women, although we are. It's that the rape and abuse being invoked is something many women have already lived through. It's a terror that lives in their bones, waiting to be activated, and anti-trans activists choose to activate it—over and over and over—because scared people are easier to manipulate. When sheer blind terror kicks in, and you start fighting like a cornered animal, reason and logic and statistics and empathy all fly out the door.

If you live in a state of chronic terror, and the people "advocating" for your "safety" don't do anything but come up with more reasons for you to be terrified, they are not your friends. They are not helping you. They are pouring gasoline on the fire, in the hopes you'll burn someone's world down, and the truth is, no one can survive living in that kind of pain forever. If the fire keeps burning, you, too, will go down in flames.

Trauma, like stigma, is a fact of life for nearly everybody. I've been in trauma therapy for the past three years, nearly as long as I've been out; my specific problem is chronic post-traumatic stress disorder, or C-PTSD, a trauma that accrues in situations of chronic, inescapable pain and abuse. The patriarchal binary *is* a situation of chronic, inescapable pain and abuse, one that was operating underneath most of the other forms of violence, abuse, or humiliation I've experienced in my lifetime. Healing is long, and slow, and requires being willing to question or challenge nearly everything about your habitual responses to the world around you. I work at it every day, and sometimes I fail.

So I don't judge anyone for having trauma, even when I hate what they do with it. Yet the cruelest quality of trauma is that it traps us in the past it is trying to protect us from. In order to stave off another attack, you continually rehearse the ones you've experienced. You compulsively scan every situation for signs that the abuse is about to happen again, and thus, you live as if you are being abused, long after the person who hurt you is gone.

Trans-eliminationist politics tell the same story that trauma tells. They are inherently fatalistic—"women" will always be victims, and "men" will always be predators, and these roles are biological, inalterable, as much a part of us as our bones. The future will always look like the past; every moment will be the moment of injury. In the absence of any hope, there is only hypervigilance and rage and the panicky need to eliminate anything that looks like a threat. It may feel, in the moment, like power—both to you and to the person you're eliminating. In fact, it is giving up all hope for a better world.

I can also tell you, having done it, that genuine healing from trauma usually consists of getting you to look around and realize all the ways you are *not* in danger—teaching your body and brain that the terrible event you are trying to protect yourself from already happened, and that it's over, and that you are still here. This is a realization many of us fight with our whole beings, because if the abuse is in the past, and we can't change the past, then we can't change what happened to us. Yet, when you internalize the fact of your own survival, your fear can no longer own you. What was pain becomes strength, in a way that is real and earned.

In order to get there, though, you have to take what feels like a terrifying leap: You have to accept that time actually does move forward, and that things will not be the same forever. In order to believe your life can get better, you have to believe that life can be *different*. You have to embrace the reality of change.

#5

GENDER AS CHANGE

"HE BECAME A MAN."

AS I SIT HERE, WRITING, IT HAS BEEN OVER FOUR YEARS since my first dose of testosterone. I have been out as trans, as a man, as a nonbinary person, for a long time; I've published books and articles under my real name; I have become a man—more or less, and there are days when it's mostly less—in the eyes of the people around me.

All this is true, and yet I still tell people I am *transitioning*. I have never slipped into the past tense. I still talk about *becoming a man*, although by any rational standard, I should say *became*. (Actually, to be perfectly on-message, I should tell you that I "was always a man." This is not true. At one point, I was a baby.) Still: I have asked myself many times what it would take for me to consider the transition over. I have wondered when I will stop becoming a man and finally just be one. Here, after long reflection, is what I've figured out:

Never. I will never finish becoming a man, and neither will any other man on the face of the planet. Our genders are not stable or fixed states of being. They are destinations, processes; "man" and "woman" are imaginary end points on a huge gender spectrum that contains every real person in existence. Gender is a goal, an end point, a role we audition for in every waking moment. No one ever exactly or entirely fits the culture's idea of "man" or "woman." Those roles are not designed for real, complex people to fit them.

No one ever becomes a man, or a woman either, because we are always in the process of becoming.

Somewhere in high school, most of us learned the paradox of Zeno's Arrow: In order to arrive at its destination, an arrow must first cover half of the distance to its target, then it covers half of the remaining distance, then half of *that* distance, and so on. If things actually work this way—which both science and logic assure us they do—no arrow should ever reach its target. It must always have 50 percent more distance to cover, even if that distance is a fraction of a millimeter of a micron thick. Arrows don't work that way, but genders do; like the protagonists of the one good Bon Jovi song, we are all only halfway there, every day of our lives.

Queer theorist Lee Edelman calls queerness a purely "negative" phenomenon. Queer isn't an actual *thing*. It's the *absence* of something, the absence of "normalcy," the failure to enact straightness or cis-ness or conformity to standard, heteronormative, patriarchal relationship and gender rules. Queer is *that which is not*, the human remainder excluded from "normal," just as woman is excluded from "man" and non-white from "white." The Other is that which our standard definition of humanity (straight, white, cis, male, rich, etc.) leaves out.[12]

Trying to fix a steady, solid, positive identity on an absence requires you to define that identity mostly in terms of suffering: *I am a woman because I experience sexism. I am gay because I endure homophobia. I am trans because people hate me for being trans.* This is risky ground on which to build anything; through this logic, our suffering becomes the essence of who we are. We can become possessive about our suffering, territorial about it, attached to it. If our moral authority derives from our victimhood, then in order to have the most authority, we also have to be the most victimized: *Trans women aren't women because they didn't experience the trauma of girlhood the way I did,* or *how could a man ever understand a woman's fear of sexual assault, let alone share it,* or *trans people who pass can't understand how hard it is to not fit into binary gender* or *people who say they're nonbinary are just cis people who want to feel special,* or *what does a straight cis woman have to complain about in terms of gender discrimination,* and the end of all these sentences is *they've got no real problems, not really, not compared to me.*

But we are not our suffering. We do not automatically become more virtuous or insightful with each ordeal. If our identities depend on the experience of oppression, then our identities depend on our oppressors—their violence defines us, and we need it in order to be righteous underdogs. I am pretty sure no one actually wants to credit abuse or oppression with making them a good person, yet we do it all the time, at least unconsciously. I do it. I am only now learning to stop.

Feminist and trans and queer movements are commonly referred to as "identity politics." Yet, to the extent that "identity" means a certain kind of politically determined suffering, these movements are actually trying to *de-identify.* "Liberation is *from* definition," writes Sarah Ahmed. "To be liberated from definition is how we open up what it is possible to do and to be."[13] *We know what we are, but we know not what we may be,* says Ophelia. An identity based on suffering is an identity based on limits.

Feminism, or queer activism, or any other form of identity politics, seeks to remove those limits and let us expand into some new shape we haven't seen yet. Underneath the structure imposed by suffering, there are people, and we have never really known—we still don't know—what people would be like if we were free.

———

TRANSNESS INTRODUCES INSTABILITY and change into the very system—gender—that is supposed to be most "natural." It turns every solid thing it touches quavery and fluid. In recent years, trans people have been cast as a threat to religion, to science, to left-wing politics, to right-wing politics, to "real" gay identity, to "real" heterosexual identity—and, yes, sometimes as a threat to feminism. Any dogmatic system of thinking about gender or identity tends to fall apart in the light of the truth that gender can change.

That uncertainty is a gift. Buddhist monk and peace activist Thich Nhat Hanh once wrote about the distinction between "knowledge" and "understanding." "Knowledge" is a belief or stance, a framework you use to make sense of your experiences. "Understanding" is simply the ability to accurately perceive the world.

"Knowledge is regarded as an obstacle for understanding," Hanh says. "If we take something to be the truth, we may cling to it so much that even if truth comes and knocks at our door, we won't want to let it in."[14]

You can hardly find a more succinct explanation for how trans people have been treated by (cis) gender experts and patriarchal authorities. All of them are so confident that they know how gender works, or how it *ought* to work, that even with trans people knocking on their doors and staring them in the face, they respond by trying to eliminate us, rather than admitting us into their picture of the world. After all: If gender doesn't work the way we're told it does, then maybe none of our assumptions about the world are valid. If our cis friends and family members haven't always known who we are, then maybe they haven't always known who *they* are, either.

Maybe they haven't. Maybe that's great. Maybe we are all—cis, trans, men, women, and everyone living in the infinitely complicated places between—so much more than we have ever been led to believe. I don't know who we are, but I know that we are not the roles imposed upon us by patriarchy—or heteronormativity, or racism, or any other system of Othering. Trans people are a threat to those systems because we are proof that no identity slapped on you from the outside can control your potential or limit your experience of the world. We can each of us be anything, so long as we are willing to change.

Uncertainty is not a threat. Uncertainty is an invitation to learn. It pushes us to discard our assumptions and engage with the world as it really exists; it can save us from our worst selves, if we let it. In a time of rising fascism, it's worth knowing that there is, in fact, a test that can successfully predict who goes Nazi—the "authoritarian personality scale," developed by Theodor Adorno after World War II—and what it tests for is nothing more nor less than the ability to tolerate ambiguity. As per *Scientific American*, the higher your tolerance for ambiguity, the less likely you are to succumb to fascist ideas.[15]

It's not just cis people who need to embrace unknowing. Just about every transgender person who has successfully come out of the closet has gone through a period of questioning everything about themselves and their lives, not knowing for certain who or what they are. To willingly change your own identity is a kind of initiation. You learn that even when nothing about you is stable, you still exist.

It has occurred to me, more than once, that I might not even be done changing—that, having gone through one radical redefinition, I may, somehow, learn even more about myself, and need to define myself all over again. This prospect used to frighten me. Now, I find it exciting—the idea that my future may hold things I cannot even imagine, that I am not done being surprised by life. I did not transition so that I could escape from one rigid, patriarchally defined gender identity into another. I did it because I wanted a life where patriarchy could not define me, a life where I would be free to be exactly myself, no matter who that was.

So I will change, because everything does; change is the story of the universe. Nothing stays still, everything is moving—every moment is in transition to the next moment is in transition to the next moment after that. Whoever I am, by the time you read this, I will not be the person who wrote it. Even the atoms that make up my body have been dirt and fish and birds and trees and other people, and when you look at it that way, the distance from female to male isn't very long at all. I will keep crossing distances; I will leave other lives and ways of being behind me. That is what I am, what you are, what life is—the act of leaving, of moving, of always becoming some other thing, until we reach the horizon and pass beyond.

ADDITIONAL READING

ONCE, IN COLLEGE, I GOT INTO A DEBATE WITH MY least favorite professor about the benefits of reading work you disagree with. The example we picked was Shakespeare; I was twenty-one years old, an age when you really do think you can cancel Shakespeare and make that stick. The professor told me that Shakespeare was relevant to everyone. I said that *no* author is relevant to everyone, and that "universality" was just code for the privileged white male viewpoint.

"What if I think Shakespeare's conception of women is misogynist," I remember asking, "and I just don't find him relevant to my life for that reason?"

"Then Shakespeare is *intensely* relevant to you," my professor said, "because you are in conflict with him. You have to read someone closely if you want to prove them wrong."

He was right—because, as much as I disliked that professor, that is the one piece of advice from college that I still think about every day.

What I've assembled here is not quite a traditional bibliography, but it *is* a useful survey of the landmarks in feminist theory and trans literature. It's not exhaustive, by any means, but if you read all of these works—I've arranged them roughly chronologically, so you can actually see the history of people disagreeing with each other and improving on each other's work—I think you would have a grasp of the major currents within each movement. I also think living a feminist life is just as important as constructing feminist theory, so I've included a section of biographical works that informed my treatment of some major figures.

You will not agree with all of these books. They don't all agree with each other, and part of the fun is figuring out which works are in conversation with each other (Andrea Long Chu's *Females* and Valerie Solanas's *SCUM Manifesto,* for example). If you're trans, I am delivering the ultimate authority into your hands—you are the only person who can draw your own lines and decide what's useful or harmful to you. Trans theory is still evolving every minute. You deserve to use all this work, whether to debunk it or to build on it, to build your own new and beautiful vision of the world.

FEMINISM

De Beauvoir, Simone: *The Second Sex,* 1949.

Solanas, Valerie: *SCUM Manifesto,* 1967.

Wittig, Monique: *Les Guérillères,* 1969, and
—*The Straight Mind: And Other Essays,* 1980.

Firestone, Shulamith: *The Dialectic of Sex: The Case for Feminist Revolution*, 1970.

Federici, Silvia: *Wages Against Housework*, 1975, and

— *Caliban and the Witch: Women, the Body, and Primitive Accumulation*, 2004.

Dinnerstein, Dorothy: *The Mermaid and the Minotaur*, 1976.

Moraga, Cherrie, and Gloria Anzaldúa, ed: *This Bridge Called My Back: Writings by Radical Women of Color*, 1981.

hooks, bell: *Feminist Theory: From Margin to Center*, 1984, and

— *All About Love: New Visions*, 1999, and

— *Feminism Is for Everybody*, 2000, and

— *The Will to Change: Men, Masculinity and Love*, 2004, and

— *We Real Cool: Black Men and Masculinity*, 2004.

Anzaldúa, Gloria: *Borderlands/La Frontera: The New Mestiza*, 1987.

Dworkin, Andrea: *Intercourse*, 1987.

Stone, Sandy: "The *Empire* Strikes Back: A Post-Transsexual Manifesto," 1987.

Stoltenberg, John: *Refusing to Be a Man: Essays on Social Justice*, 1989.

Herman, Judith: *Trauma and Recovery: The Aftermath of Violence—From Domestic Abuse to Political Terror*, 1992.

Connell, Raewyn: *Masculinities*, 1995.

Elliott, Beth (as Geri Nettick): *Mirrors: Portrait of a Lesbian Transsexual*, 1996.

Kaplan, Laura: *The Story of Jane: The Legendary Underground Feminist Abortion Service*, 1996.

Roberts, Dorothy: *Killing the Black Body: Race, Reproduction and the Meaning of Liberty*, 1997.

Serano, Julia: *Whipping Girl: A Transsexual Woman on Sexism and the Scapegoating of Femininity*, 2007, and

— *Excluded: Making Feminist and Queer Movements More Inclusive*, 2013.

Ward, Jane: *Not Gay: Sex Between Straight White Men*, 2015, and

— *The Tragedy of Heterosexuality*, 2020.

Ross, Loretta J., and Rickie Solinger: *Reproductive Justice: An Introduction*, 2017.

McBee, Thomas Page: *Amateur: A True Story About What Makes a Man*, 2018.

Smith, Molly and Juno Mac: *Revolting Prostitutes: The Fight for Sex Workers' Rights*, 2018.

O'Brien, M. E.: *Family Abolition: Capitalism and the Communizing of Care*, 2023.

Saini, Angela: *The Patriarchs: The Origins of Inequality*, 2023.

Heaney, Emma, ed.: *Feminism Against Cisness*, 2024.

TRANS/GENDER BASICS

Butler, Judith: *Gender Trouble: Feminism and the Subversion of Identity*, 1989, and

— *Bodies That Matter: On the Discursive Limits of "Sex,"* 1993, and

—*Who's Afraid of Gender?*, 2024.

Stryker, Susan: "My Words to Victor Frankenstein Above the Village of Chamounix," 1993, and

— *Transgender History*, 2008, and

— (with Dylan McCarthy Blackston, ed.) *The Transgender Studies Reader Remix*, 2022.

Feinberg, Leslie: *Stone Butch Blues*, 1993, and

— *Transgender Warriors: Making History from Joan of Arc to Dennis Rodman*, 1996, and

— *Trans Liberation: Beyond Pink or Blue*, 1998.

Bornstein, Kate: *Gender Outlaw: On Men, Women and the Rest of Us*, 1994.

Cameron, Loren: *Body Alchemy: Transsexual Portraits*, 1996.

Oyěwùmí, Oyèrónkẹ́: *The Invention of Women: Making an African Sense of Western Gender Discourses*, 1997.

Halberstam, Jack: *Female Masculinity*, 1998.

Rubin, Henry: *Self-Made Men: Identity and Embodiment Among Transsexual Men*, 2003.

Green, Jamison: *Becoming a Visible Man*, 2004.

Valerio, Max Wolf: *The Testosterone Files: My Hormonal and Social Transformation from Female to Male*, 2006.

Spade, Dean: *Normal Life: Administrative Violence, Critical Trans Politics and the Limits of Law*, 2011.

Binnie, Imogen: *Nevada*, 2013.

Mock, Janet: *Redefining Realness: My Path to Womanhood, Identity, Love & So Much More*, 2014.

McBee, Thomas Page: *Man Alive: A True Story of Violence, Forgiveness & Becoming a Man*, 2014.

Kaveney, Roz: *Tiny Pieces of Skull*, 2015.

Snorton, C. Riley: *Black on Both Sides: A Racial History of Trans Identity*, 2017.

Gill-Peterson, Jules: *Histories of the Transgender Child*, 2018.

Chu, Andrea Long: *Females*, 2019.

Rajunov, Micah, and Scott Duane: *Nonbinary: Memoirs of Gender and Identity*, 2019.

Sullivan, Lou: *We Both Laughed in Pleasure: Selected Diaries of Lou Sullivan*, 2019.

Abi-Karam, Andrea, and Kay Gabriel, ed: *We Want It All: An Anthology of Radical Trans Poetics*, 2020.

Faye, Shon: *The Transgender Issue: An Argument for Justice*, 2021.

Awkward-Rich, Cameron: *The Terrible We: Thinking with Trans Maladjustment*, 2022.

Heyam, Kit: *Before We Were Trans: A New History of Gender,* 2022.

Griffin-Gracy, Miss Major, and Toshio Maronek: *Miss Major Speaks: Conversations with a Black Trans Revolutionary,* 2023.

Ashley, Florence: *Gender/Fucking: The Pleasures and Politics of Living in a Gendered Body,* 2024.

BIOGRAPHICAL SOURCES

Andrea Dworkin

Duberman, Martin: *Andrea Dworkin: The Feminist as Revolutionary*, 2020.

Dworkin, Andrea: *Heartbreak: The Political Memoir of a Feminist Militant*, 2002.

Shulamith Firestone

Faludi, Susan: "Death of a Revolutionary," *The New Yorker*, 2013.

Firestone, Shulamith: *Airless Spaces*, 1993.

bell hooks

hooks, bell: *Bone Black: Memories of Girlhood*, 1996, and

— *Wounds of Passion: A Writing Life*, 1997.

Nittle, Nadra: *bell hooks' spiritual vision: Buddhist, Christian and Feminist*, 2023.

Pauli Murray

Murray, Pauli: *Song in a Weary Throat: Memoir of an American Pilgrimage*, 1987.

Rosenberg, Rosalind: *Jane Crow: The Life of Pauli Murray*, 2017.

ACKNOWLEDGMENTS

One of the most important shifts for me, since coming out as trans, is that I've stopped writing so much as an individual and learned to write as a member of a community. This book would be nothing without its interviewees, each of whom added immeasurable knowledge and perspective to the book. Some of the best and most informative interviews weren't directly quoted, so please read the whole list: C. N. Lester, Cristan Williams, Devon Price, Emily St. James, Emma Heaney, Florence Ashley, Gillian Branstetter, Jane Ward, Jay Edidin, John Stoltenberg, Jos Truitt, Julia Serano, Kit Heyam, Ky Schevers, Max Wolf Valerio, Raewyn Connell, Roz Kaveney, and Simon D. Elin Fisher. To Audrey, in particular, for trusting me with her story, my profound thanks.

Inigo Purcell and Maddox K. Pennington were also interviewed for this book, but, more importantly, they were the first transmasculine people I spoke to when I was figuring my own shit out. My profound gratitude to them, from that day to this.

I'm able to write, and to be who I am, because of all the trans men and transmasculine people who were writing and advocating for our community long before I came along—I've tried to credit as many as possible by name, but I want to explicitly own the debt, once more, just to be on the safe side. I'm also deeply indebted to the work of bell hooks, who taught me how to write from the inside and the outside of a movement simultaneously—how to be critical of feminism while still loving it, and vice versa.

To the editors who saved this book from an exceptionally messy first draft, Amber Qureshi and Michelle Capone, my thanks. And thanks, once again, to everyone at Melville House, which has always been a fantastically supportive and trustworthy home for my nonfiction.

Many thanks to my agent, Melissa Flashman, who has stuck with me through no end of weird projects and pitches.

To my husband, Brian, who received the ultimate weird pitch from me in the form of our continued marriage—I love you and I'm grateful for you. Also, thanks for pretending to be gay for me, buddy! It's been a long con, undertaken for no specific purpose, but as long as no one reads the acknowledgments of this book, I think we'll pull it off.

To my child: You are the best and funniest and kindest person I have ever met. You are such a wonderful kid that I am astonished that I get to raise you. Every day, I love you a little bit more, so as I write this, I love you more than I have ever loved you—and, whoever you are by the time you read this, I will love you even more.

ENDNOTES

INTRODUCTION

1   *The Terrible We*, Cameron Awkward-Rich, p. 87.

2   *Amateur*, Thomas Page McBee, p. 110.

3   *The Transsexual Empire*, Janice Raymond, p. xiii–xiv.

4   *The Dialectic of Sex*, Shulamith Firestone, Ch. 1.

5   *Borderlands/La Frontera*, Gloria Anzaldúa, p. 89, p. 33.

PART 1

1   *The Argonauts*, Maggie Nelson, p. 52.

2   Tia Ghosh, "Viking Warrior Presumed to Be a Man Is Actually a Woman," LiveScience, September 14, 2017, https://www.livescience.com/60418-viking-warrior-was-a-woman.html.

3   *Wisconsin Death Trip*, Michael Lesy, p. 130, p. 99.

4   *Whipping Girl*, Julia Serano, p. 88.

5   Laura Dodsworth, "The Detransitioners," Medium, August 18, 2020, https://web.archive.org/web/20210312171613/ https://medium.com/@barereality/the-detransitioners-72a4e01a10f9.

6   J. K. Rowling, "J.K. Rowling Writes About Her Reasons for Speaking Out on Sex and Gender Issues," jkrowling.com, June 10 2020, https://www.jkrowling.com/opinions/j-k-rowling-writes-about-her-reasons-for-speaking-out-on-sex-and-gender-issues/.

7   "'Female Socialization' is a Transphobic Myth," Devon Price, PhD, Medium, 8/2/21, https://medium.com/p/97747d1c7fb2.

8   *The Empusium*, Olga Tokarczuk, p. 128.

9   Lil Kalish, "A 25-Year-Old Trans Activist Injected Testosterone In Front of the Florida Board of Medicine To Protest a Ban On Gender-Affirming Care for Minors," BuzzFeed News, February 13, 2023, https://www.buzzfeednews.com/article/lilkalish/trans-activist-injects-testosterone-florida-medicine-meeting.

10 "Only 5 Days into the Year, 125 Anti-Trans Bills Have Been Filed," Erin Reed, Erin In The Morning, January 5, 2024, https://www.erininthemorning.com/p/only-5-days-into-the-year-125-anti.

11 "Senate passes defense bill that includes ban on gender-affirming care for minors," Alexandra Marquez, NBC News, December 18, 2024, https://www.nbcnews.com/politics/congress/senate-passes-defense-bill-ban-gender-affirming-care-minors-rcna184748.

12 "Protecting Children from Chemical and Surgical Mutilation: Executive Order," Donald Trump, White House, January 28, 2025, https://www.whitehouse.gov/presidential-actions/2025/01/protecting-children-from-chemical-and-surgical-mutilation/.

13 "Many States Are Trying to Restrict Gender Treatments for Adults, Too," Azeen Ghorayshi, *New York Times*, April 22, 2023, https://www.nytimes.com/2023/04/22/health/transgender-adults-treatment-bans.html.

14 "Ohio, Michigan Republicans in Released Audio: 'Endgame' Is to Ban Trans Care 'for Everyone,'" Erin Reed, Erin in the Morning, January 27, 2024, https://www.erininthemorning.com/p/ohio-michigan-republicans-in-released.

15 *Whipping Girl*, Julia Serano, p. 135.

16 *The Transgender* Issue, Shon Faye, p. 83.

17 *The Story of Jane*, Laura Kaplan, p. xxii, p. 38, p. 22.

18 The Patriarchs, Angela Saini, p. 26.

19 "Narrative of the Captivity and Restoration of Mrs. Mary Rowlandson," Mary Rowlandson, Ch. 20, https://www.gutenberg.org/files/851/851-h/851-h.htm.

20 *Sisters in Spirit: Haudenosaunee (Iroquois) Influence on Early American Feminists*, Sally Roesch Wagner, Ch. 3.

21 *The Sacred Hoop*, Paula Gunn Allen, p. 195, p. 40.

22 "Defending Women From Gender Ideology Extremism and Restoring Biological Truth To The Federal Government: Executive Order," Donald Trump, WhiteHouse.gov, January 20, 2025, https://www.whitehouse.gov/presidential-

actions/2025/01/defending-women-from-gender-ideology-
extremism-and-restoring-biological-truth-to-the-federal-
government/.

23 *The Patriarchs*, Angela Saini, p. 40.

24 *The Invention of Women*, Oyèrónkẹ́ Oyěwùmí, p. 29.

25 *Queer (In)justice*, Joey L. Mogul, Andrea J. Ritchie and Kay
Whitlock, p.1.

26 "Two Spirits, One Heart, Five Genders," Duane Brayboy,
ICT News, September 7, 2017 https://ictnews.org/archive/
two-spirits-one-heart-five-genders#:~:text=George%20
Catlin%20said%20that%20the,Native%20beliefs%20
and%20history%2C%20including.

PART 2

1 "I went on a date with Aziz Ansari. It turned into the worst
night of my life," Katie Way, Babe.Net, January 13, 2018,
https://babe.net/2018/01/13/aziz-ansari-28355.

2 *Tess of the D'Urbervilles*, Thomas Hardy, Chapter 11, https://
www.gutenberg.org/files/110/110-h/110-h.htm#chap11.

3 "Baby, It's Cold Outside," Genius.com, https://genius.com/
Idina-menzel-baby-its-cold-outside-lyrics.

4 *Intercourse*, Andrea Dworkin, p. 175.

5 *The Tragedy of Heterosexuality*, Jane Ward, p. 35, p. 33–34,
p. 36.

6 *Not Gay: Sex Between Straight White Men*, Jane Ward, p. 55.

7   *The Tragedy of Heterosexuality*, Jane Ward, p. 39, p. 40,
     p. 30.

8   *The Straight Mind*, Monique Witting, p. 32.

9   "Sexual Assault in the Transgender Community," Office
     for Victims of Crime, https://ovc.ojp.gov/sites/g/files/
     xyckuh226/files/pubs/forge/sexual_numbers.html#victims.

PART 3

1   "Death of a Revolutionary," Susan Faludi, *The New
     Yorker*, April 8, 2013, https://www.newyorker.com/
     magazine/2013/04/15/death-of-a-revolutionary.

2   *The Dialectic of Sex*, Shulamith Firestone, Ch. 4, Ch. 10, Ch.
     1, Ch. 10.

3   "Everything you need to know about artificial wombs," MIT
     Technology Review, Cassandra Willard, September 29, 2023,
     https://www.technologyreview.com/2023/09/29/1080538/
     everything-you-need-to-know-about-artificial-wombs.

4   "Republicans block Senate bill to protect nationwide access
     to IVF treatments," PBS NewsHour, Mary Clare Jalonick
     and Stephen Groves, February 28, 2024, https://www.pbs.
     org/newshour/politics/republicans-block-senate-bill-to-
     protect-nationwide-access-to-ivf-treatments.

5   "Frozen Embryos are the New Orphan Crisis," *Christianity
     Today*, Kara Bettis Carvalho, November 20, 2023, https://
     www.christianitytoday.com/ct/2023/december/ivf-frozen-
     embryos-are-new-orphan-crisis.html.

6   "The Pimping of Pregnancy," juliebindel.substack.com, Julie
      Bindel, May 10, 2023, https://juliebindel.substack.com/p/
      the-pimping-of-pregnancy.

7   *Airless Spaces*, Shulamith Firestone, p. 130.

8   *The Dialectic of Sex*, Shulamith Firestone, Ch. 1.

9   *Caliban and the Witch*, Silvia Federici, p. 111.

10   *Histories of the Transgender Child*, Jules Gill-Peterson, p. 93.

11   "Cold War Pavlov: Homosexual aversion therapy in
      the 1960s," *History of the Human Sciences*, Vol. 34,
      Issue 1, Kate Davison, https://journals.sagepub.com/
      doi/10.1177/0952695120911593.

12   "Conversion Therapy and LGBT Youth," UCLA School of
      Law Williams Institute, June 2019, https://williamsinstitute.
      law.ucla.edu/publications/conversion-therapy-and-lgbt-
      youth/.

13   "Trans conversion therapy survivor: 'I was strapped to a
      chair and given painful electric shocks,'" *The Standard*,
      Emma Loffhagen, April 29, 2022, https://www.standard.
      co.uk/lifestyle/trans-conversion-therapy-survivors-lgbt-
      government-b994469.html.

14   *Trans America: A Counter-History*, Barry Reay https://
      books.google.com/books?id=R1biDwAAQBAJ&pg
      =PT70&lpg=PT70&dq=%22nonetheless,+americ
      an+trans+people+did+seek+out+surgery%22&sou
      rce=bl&ots=gj-MRvGZeG&sig=ACfU3U3TqPMe-
      c50KzZzguPecLdcfMhvV-
      g&hl=en&sa=X&ved=2ahUKEwiYrNvk-8mFA-U9M1k

FHfwUA3oQ6AF6BAgJEAM#v=onepage&q=%22none
theless%2C%20american%20trans%20people%20did%20
seek%20out%20surgery%22&f=false.

15 "Kenneth Zucker vs. Transgender People," Transgender
    Map, https://www.transgendermap.com/issues/psychology/
    kenneth-zucker/.

16 "Characteristics of perpetrators of child maltreatment,"
    Office of Juvenile Justice and Delinquency Prevention,
    https://ojjdp.ojp.gov/statistical-briefing-book/victims/faqs/
    qa02111.

17 "The Gender Pay Gap Is Largely Because of Motherhood,"
    Claire Cain Miller, *The New York Times*, May 13, 2017,
    https://www.nytimes.com/2017/05/13/upshot/the-gender-
    pay-gap-is-largely-because-of-motherhood.html.

18 "Gender Quit Gap Widest in States with Most Child Care
    Breakdowns," Jane Fillion, First Five Years Fund, February
    18, 2022, https://www.ffyf.org/resources/2022/02/gender-
    quit-gap-widest-in-states-with-most-child-care-breakdowns/.

19 "Women provided 3 times more child care than men during
    pandemic, analysis finds," Katie Kindelman, ABC News,
    June 25, 2021, https://abcnews.go.com/GMA/Living/
    women-provided-times-child-care-men-pandemic-analysis/
    story?id=78464559.

20 "Nearly Half of Men Say They Do Most of the Home
    Schooling. 3 Percent of Women Agree," Claire Cain Miller,
    The New York Times, May 6, 2020, https://www.nytimes.
    com/2020/05/06/upshot/pandemic-chores-homeschooling-
    gender.html.

21 "Research Shows Moms with Husbands or Live-In Male Partners Do More Housework Than Single Moms," Population Reference Bureau, May 8, 2019, https://www.prb.org/news/mothers-day/.

22 *Touched Out*, Amanda Montei, p. 71.

23 "The Road to TERFdom," *Lux* Magazine, Katie Baker, April 13, 2021, https://lux-magazine.com/article/the-road-to-terfdom/.

24 *The Dialectic of Sex*, Shulamith Firestone, Ch. 1.

25 *The Transsexual Empire*, Janice Raymond, p. xiii, p. 27.

26 "'An explosion': what is behind the rise in girls questioning their gender identity?" Amelia Gentleman, *The Guardian*, November 24, 2022 https://www.theguardian.com/society/2022/nov/24/an-explosion-what-is-behind-the-rise-in-girls-questioning-their-gender-identityhttps://www.theguardian.com/society/2022/nov/24/an-explosion-what-is-behind-the-rise-in-girls-questioning-their-gender-identity.

27 *Irreversible Damage*, Abigail Shrier, p. 31, p. 211–215, p. 201, p. 31.

28 *Before We Were Trans*, Kit Heyam, p. 16–17.

29 "About 5% of young adults in the U.S. say their gender is different from their sex assigned at birth," Pew Research Center, Anna Brown, June 7, 2022, https://www.pewresearch.org/short-reads/2022/06/07/about-5-of-young-adults-in-the-u-s-say-their-gender-is-different-from-their-sex-assigned-at-birth/.

30 *Reproductive Justice: An Introduction*, Loretta J. Ross and Rickie Solinger, p. 18.

31 *Killing the Black Body*, Dorothy Roberts, p. 12.

32 *How All Politics Became Reproductive Politics*, Laura Briggs, p. 16.

33 *Reproductive Justice: An Introduction*, Loretta J. Ross & Rickie Solinger, p. 51–52

34 "The Sweat and Blood of Fannie Lou Hamer," National Endowment for the Humanities, Rosalind Early, Winter 2021, https://www.neh.gov/article/sweat-and-blood-fannie-lou-hamer.

35 Reproductive Justice: An Introduction, Loretta J. Ross & Rickie Solinger, p. 31.

36 "*The Atlantic* tried to artistically show gender dysphoria on its cover. Instead it damaged the trust of transgender readers," Poynter, Sydney Bauer, September 4, 2020, https://www.poynter.org/ethics-trust/2020/the-atlantic-tried-artistically-show-gender-dysphoria-cover-instead-damaged-trust-transgender-readers/.

37 Laura Dodsworth, "The Detransitioners," Medium, August 18, 2020, https://web.archive.org/web/20210312171613/https://medium.com/@barereality/the-detransitioners-72a4e01a10f9.

38 "Despite Endless Corporate Propaganda, Black Youth are Not Transitioning," The Transgender Medical Scandal, Alix Aharon, https://web.archive.org/web/20210616122314/

https://www.gendermapper.org/post/despite-endless-corporate-propaganda-black-youth-are-not-transitioning.

39 *Bone Black*, bell hooks, p. 30, p. 99, p. 102.

40 *All About Love*, bell hooks, p. 21.

41 *Feminist Theory: From Margin to Center*, bell hooks, p. 38.

42 *Feminism is for Everybody*, bell hooks, p. xiv.

43 *Feminist Theory: From Margin to Center*, bell hooks, p. 118.

44 *All About Love*, bell hooks, p. 6–8, p. 29.

45 "Notes on the House of Bondage," *The Nation*, James Baldwin, November 1, 1980, https://www.thenation.com/article/archive/notes-house-bondage/.

46 "the times," Lucille Clifton, as republished in *The New York Times*, December 10, 2020, https://www.nytimes.com/2020/12/10/magazine/poem-the-times.html.

47 *Feminist Theory: From Margin to Center*, bell hooks, p. 145.

48 "Parents of Daniel Aston, bartender killed at Club Q, reflect on year without their son," Claire Lavezzorio, Denver News 7, November 18, 2023, https://www.denver7.com/news/club-q-shooting/parents-of-daniel-aston-bartender-killed-at-club-q-reflect-on-year-without-their-son.

PART 4

1 "Andrea Dworkin: Biological Essentialism vs. Political Materialism," Janice Raymond, *Women Are Human*, November 2, 2021, https://web.archive.org/

web/20211103024534/https://www.womenarehuman.com/andrea-dworkin-biological-essentialism-vs-political-materialism/.

2   *Woman Hating*, Andrea Dworkin, p. 148.

3   "Andrea Dworkin Was a Trans Ally," John Stoltenberg, *Boston Review*, April 8, 2020, https://www.bostonreview.net/articles/john-stoltenberg-andrew-dworkin-was-trans-ally/.

4   *Woman Hating*, Andrea Dworkin, p. 148.

5   "We All Need a Gender Off-Ramp," John Stoltenberg, An Injustice!, April 11, 2021, https://aninjusticemag.com/we-all-need-a-gender-off-ramp-ceb5006b864.

6   *Transgender History*, Susan Stryker, p. 104.

7   *Mirrors*, Beth Elliott, p. 258.

8   "How a Feminist, Lesbian Music Collective Powerfully Defended Trans Rights in 1970s Los Angeles," Felix Moore, *Pink News*, April 24, 2023, https://www.thepinknews.com/2023/04/24/sandy-stone-olivia-records-trans-rights-los-angeles/.

9   "Robin Morgan Slanders Beth Elliott," *The Berkeley Revolution*, https://revolution.berkeley.edu/robin-morgan-slanders-beth-elliot/#menu-main-nav.

10   "The Conversations Project," Cristan Williams, TransAdvocate, http://radfem.transadvocate.com/the-conversations-project/.

11   *The Transsexual Empire*, Janice Raymond, p. 178, p. 102–104.

12   *Mirrors*, Beth Elliott, p. 228, p. 189, p. 183–184.

13   *Heartbreak*, Andrea Dworkin, p. 152.

14   "J. K. Rowling Writes about Her Reasons for Speaking out on Sex and Gender Issues," J.K. Rowling, JKRowling.com, https://www.jkrowling.com/opinions/j-k-rowling-writes-about-her-reasons-for-speaking-out-on-sex-and-gender-issues/.

15   J. K. Rowling, X.com, https://x.com/jk_rowling.

16   "Ben Appel In Spiked about the New Homophobia," Mumsnet, May 14, 2023, https://www.mumsnet.com/talk/womens_rights/4805830-ben-appel-in-spiked-about-the-new-homophobia.

17   *Self-Made Men*, Henry Rubin, p. 124.

18   "Masculinity Crisis: How It Feels When You Start to Look Like Them," Oliver Reeson, The Lifted Brow, December 2, 2019, https://web.archive.org/web/20191203173126/https://www.theliftedbrow.com/liftedbrow/2019/12/2/masculinity-crisis-how-it-feels-when-you-start-to-look-like-them-by-oliver-reeson.

19   *Refusing to Be a Man*, John Stoltenberg, p. xiii, p. xi, p. 22–23, p. 44.

20   "Andrea Dworkin Was Not Transphobic," Medium, John Stoltenberg, April 18, 2021, https://johnstoltenberg.medium.com/andrea-dworkin-was-not-transphobic-6f4f94bdf4a1.

21   "The Unforgivable Transing of Andrea Dworkin," Julie Bindel, Julie Bindel Substack, January 10, 2024, https://juliebindel.substack.com/p/the-unforgivable-transing-of-andrea.

22   "Woke Andrea Dworkin," Phyllis Chesler, *Tablet* Magazine,

April 9, 2021, https://www.tabletmag.com/sections/arts-letters/articles/woke-andrea-dworkin

23 "Andrea Dworkin: Biological Essentialism vs. Political Materialism," Janice Raymond, Women Are Human, November 2, 2021, https://www.womenarehuman.com/andrea-dworkin-biological-essentialism-vs-political-materialism/.

24 "We All Need a Gender Off-Ramp," An Injustice!, John Stoltenberg, April 11, 2021, https://aninjusticemag.com/we-all-need-a-gender-off-ramp-ceb5006b864.

25 "Review Article: Dworkin's Mercy," Roz Kaveney, *Feminist Review* No. 38 (Summer 1991), https://www.jstor.org/stable/1395380.

26 *Amateur*, Thomas Page McBee, p. 48, p. 50.

PART 5

1 Gillian Branstetter, Bluesky.com, November 5, 2024, https://bsky.app/profile/gbbranstetter.bsky.social/post/3la7vs6zipd2s.

2 "AP VoteCast: About half of voters said support for transgender rights has gone too far," Amelia Thomson-Deveaux, Associated Press, November 5, 2024 https://apnews.com/live/trump-harris-election-updates-11-5-2024%C2%A0?tab=00000192-dde3-df8c-a7fb-fdeb0f780000#00000192-ffbf-dc56-a39e-ffbf5c030000.

3 Nicholas J. Fuentes, X.com, November 5, 2024, https://x.com/NickJFuentes/status/1854015641218355621.

4   "LGBT Identification in U.S. Ticks Up to 7.1%," Jeffrey M. Jones, Gallup, February 17, 2022, https://news.gallup.com/poll/389792/lgbt-identification-ticks-up.aspx.

5   QuickFacts, United States Census, https://www.census.gov/quickfacts/fact/table/US/LFE046222.

6   *Some Styles of Masculinity*, Gregg Bordowitz, p. 218–219.

7   *Jane Crow: The Life of Pauli Murray*, Rosalind Rosenberg, p. 138.

8   *Transgender Studies Reader Remix*, ed. Susan Stryker and Dylan McCarthy Johnston, p. 557–558.

9   *Andrea Dworkin: The Feminist as Revolutionary*, Martin Duberman, p. 265.

10 "More than 40% of transgender adults in the US have attempted suicide," UCLA School of Law Williams Institute, July 20, 2023, https://williamsinstitute.law.ucla.edu/press/transpop-suicide-press-release/.

11 "Trauma, Discrimination and PTSD Among LGBTQ+ People," Sarah E. Valentine, PhD, Nicholas A. Livingston, PhD, Anna C. Salomaa, PhD, and Jillian C. Shipherd, PhD, PTSD: National Center for PTSD, https://www.ptsd.va.gov/professional/treat/specific/trauma_discrimination_lgbtq.asp.

12 The Edelman book I am summing up—inexpertly!—is *Bad Education*.

13 "Define Women! And Other Patriarchal Instructions," Sarah Ahmed, Feminist Killjoys, July 10, 2024, https://feministkilljoys.com/2024/07/10/define-women-and-other-patriarchal-instructions/.

14   *Awakening the Heart: Essential Buddhist Sutras and Commentaries*, Thich Nhat Hanh, p, 414–415.

15   "Election Grief Is Real. Here's How to Cope," Meghan Bartels, *Scientific American*, November 6, 2024, https://www.scientificamerican.com/article/election-grief-is-real-heres-how-to-cope/.

Jude Ellison S. Doyle is the author of *Trainwreck: The Women We Love to Hate, Mock, and Fear . . . and Why* and *Dead Blondes and Bad Mothers: Monstrosity, Patriarchy, and the Fear of Female Power.* He is also the author of the graphic novels *Maw SC* and *The Neighbors.* His work has appeared in *In These Times, The Guardian, Elle.com, The Atlantic, Slate, Buzzfeed,* and *Rookie,* among other publications. He is the founder of the blog Tiger Beatdown. He lives in Brooklyn, New York.